Odd Man Out

A PLAYER'S DIARY

Brian McClair

with Joyce Woolridge

First published in Great Britain in 1997
This edition published in 1998
by **Manchester United Books**
an imprint of **VCI plc**
76 Dean Street, London W1V 5HA
(www.vci.co.uk)
in association with
Manchester United Football Club plc
Old Trafford, Manchester M16 ORA

CIP data for this title is available from the British Library

ISBN 0 233 99362 2

1 2 3 4 5 6 7 8 9 10

 A Zone production

Designed by **offspring** for **Zone**
Photos by **Action Images, Rob Wilson, John Peters, Empics, Allsport**

Printed by **McKays of Chatham plc**, Kent

Contents

Acknowledgements

Justyn Barnes

Lou Pepper

Nicky Paris

Tim Barnes

Carol Briggs

David Hicks

Tim Forrester

James Freedman

Anna Kiernan

PROLOGUE

Pre-season, August, 1996

As I arrive at Old Trafford after what has been a particularly painful training session following the summer break, I'm met by a familiar scene. Though the season has not yet begun, the area around the stadium is swarming with fans who have come, not to see a match, but to shop at the Megastore, visit the museum or queue for the ground tour. Because it's around lunch time, most people are hoping to catch players who have spent the morning at the Cliff, Manchester United's training ground. They're ready to take photographs or get an autograph. Over the ten years I've been a player at this club, I've seen these crowds grow bigger and bigger: these supporters desperately want to take part in whatever way they can in the success the team has achieved.

1996/97 is my testimonial season. It's also the last year of my current contract. In my career here I've been described in a variety of terms, from "the most underrated player at United" to "Lord of the Pies". My favourite has to be this description from a letter to a fanzine, just packed with protest and truth: "My armchair is a better player than Brian McClair."

This is the problem with being what is fashionably known as "a squad player". Everyone sagely agrees that the pressure on top clubs means professionals in this country should ape the continentals in accepting they may not be an automatic first-team choice, as a large squad is essential for success. But those of us who find ourselves in this position are derided as lacking in ambition or greedy and lazy if we don't immediately slap our transfer request on the manager's desk. It was very difficult for me when I first started to be left out; I had played constantly for Motherwell and Celtic, and only occasionally suffered being dropped. It took me a whole year to sort it out in my mind. All the time you have to think: "What are the positive things about staying at United? What are the positive and negative things about going somewhere else?" I can't speak for others who find themselves in the same situation at other clubs, but for me, continuing to be involved here has been and is still my ultimate aim. I know I've served a purpose at Old Trafford. Even when I was a younger player and commentators used to say I could walk into most of the other teams in the Premiership, remaining at United was a token of my ambition and not the sign of a lack of it. If I could have done anything to change what was happening to me, I would have done it; but I wanted to stay here. Therefore I've had to get on with whatever the job is, to be fit and ready to play, and to play when I have the chance – whether in the Reserves, in friendlies or pre-season tournaments, or in the last 10 minutes of a Premiership game.

Despite the fact that I'm supposed to have been on my way to Bolton, Bury and other assorted places over the last close season, here I am still. I move slowly through the crowd towards the Reception area, signing books and programmes (probably illegibly). The automatic door flies open and the receptionist behind the counter announces, "Hello, Brian, we're seeing a lot of you at the moment." "Indeed," I answer, "I'm determined to make the most of my last season here." She isn't sure what expression to adopt. I move on through the inner door that only the chosen few are allowed to pass and into the complex of rooms, offices and restaurants which flank the tunnel. In the stairwell are bags of mail for some players. None of the grey, bulging sacks is for me. I have a storage box nearby which is sufficient for the loyal band of admirers who have aged gracefully with me, though recently my post has been swelled by letters generated by my regular feature for the Manchester United Magazine, "Choccy's Diary", which has been described as a masterpiece of understatement (or, by the manager, as the product of the strange way in which my mind works).

David Beckham trundles past me, weighted down by the two heavy bags he's delivering to the secretaries for franking and posting. I'm reminded forcibly how differently things are done here. When I first came to Manchester in 1987, I had to deal with far more post than I'd ever had before. I assumed that the system was the same as it had been at Celtic, where you paid for everything yourself. I'd go out and buy stamps and envelopes because it just didn't occur to me to do anything else. It wasn't for quite some time that I discovered you could get stationery free from the club and that they pay for postage. You also receive the photographs free which you send out signed. At Celtic you had to buy them from the club; here they give you hundreds at a time, though I usually need only five or six. Steve Bruce came back from Birmingham a few days ago and pointed out some other differences between United and elsewhere, like not having to pay for your own lunch. As I've played for other clubs I have known other ways of doing things, but I expect this would come as a surprise to the young players who have only ever been here.

Obviously, this account of the season won't tell you what it's like to struggle to make ends meet at the bottom of the lower Leagues. I will, instead, be trying to show you what it is like to play football in the highly privileged setting of what I have no doubt is the biggest club in England, and all that goes with it. Though Manchester United has come to be seen as a monstrous example of financial greed and arrogance, its glamour, its history and its wealth are as vital a part of the story of football in this country as anything else. Just as United is not a typical club, I'm often seen as an atypical player, because I began a degree, have left-wing politics and read books. Perhaps I am therefore well suited to the task of telling the story of life at this far from ordinary place.

1

Kits and Starts

"Someone has to wear the padded kit..."

In the summer of 1996, we were all badly in need of a rest after chasing a second double. The stress builds up to something close to an unbearable level when you're near to winning something. It surprised me that it doesn't get any easier the more it happens. 1995/96 was a long, hard campaign, spending so much time with the squad, training with each other every day. It's a wonder that we managed to avoid getting on each others' nerves too badly. I've heard it said that footballers don't suffer stress, or shouldn't, bearing in mind that they are paid high wages for doing something they love. It's an interesting viewpoint but completely wrong. Physical recovery is easy but the mental strain doesn't disappear so quickly.

There are well-known, high-profile cases of what stress can do and what players have turned to in order to cope. For players who don't go to those extremes, the symptoms of stress (if they are anything like mine) are constant irritability and bad temper. It means I'm not a very pleasant person to be with. And there is nowhere you can go to relax your nerves for a few hours. If you go out for a meal, to the pictures, to the pub or for a day out with your family, everyone wants to talk to you about football. Football serves as a displacement activity for millions in this country and elsewhere, but it can't be mine. I hope that I manage stress better than when I was a younger man. It's surprisingly difficult to recognize that the reason you are losing your temper is because of the strain that your football is putting upon you. There were times in my career when I found things very hard to cope with, but what has sustained me is that even the worst of times in a professional footballer's life would be a dream come true for most people and that, if I hadn't pulled on a football shirt, I would now be a mathematics teacher.

I've been named by Keith Gillespie as the worst at training in the club, but the arrival of Jordi Cruyff as one of the summer signings looks like depriving me of this honour. I spend my time trying not to line up next to one of the many underdeveloped youths who now populate the first team, as my mature figure is something of a contrast. I suppose someone has to wear the padded kit.

At the end of July, we began our carefully designed programme of pre-season games in Ireland, where we have an enormous and dedicated following and where our players love to visit. The matches were enjoyable and relaxed, but still competitive. However, the pace soon picked up with the start of the Umbro tournament in the first week of August.

It would be fruitless to claim that the point of this competition, between United, Ajax and Nottingham Forest, was anything other than to meet the purposes of the sponsors. But it was probably better preparation for the new season than a tour of the Continent or farther afield, which would involve exhausting, continuous travel. Since our recent success, pre-season matches have begun to resemble triumphal progresses, but we need testing matches against strong teams. We used to go frequently to Scandinavia, before their football improved. It was hardly worth the trouble of putting on your boots for games which we'd win 7–0.

High temperatures at the City Ground meant that we didn't escape one of the problems of touring abroad. Another difficulty was that the matches were too close together to allow players to recover properly, but they served their purpose. The tournament even gave me the opportunity to score two goals. We lost the first tie to Ajax by a late winner, but I managed to score our only goal after Peter Schmeichel launched a blooter up the park which was headed on and came across to me. I had the good fortune to be up against Danny Blind, who is obligingly six inches shorter than me, which allowed me to stretch for the ball with my left foot and push it past the keeper. In the knife-edge play-off against Nottingham Forest for third place, I scored again. I was in the right place at the right time and knocked in one of those goals which fans are always telling you anyone, even an armchair, could score. We won 3–1.

A few days later, we found ourselves in the even more glamorous surroundings of the San Siro for the first of two matches against Inter Milan as part of Paul Ince's transfer. Just as against Ajax, we were reminded of what it takes to be successful in Europe, and it was a good lesson for the younger players who hadn't experienced this before. We played well enough, but were punished for a failure to concentrate. After half time we lost two goals suddenly. I've played in many European games and have to say that United has been constantly guilty of committing that mistake: you can be congratulating yourself that everything is going well and in five minutes you've conceded two goals and the game is effectively over.

Foreign travel would appear to be one of the perks of the job. Well, we stayed in an extremely comfortable hotel but saw very little of the city, and this is our usual experience. We were eaten alive by mosquitoes; David Fevre, our physio, held the record for the number of bites.

Our pre-season warm-up peaked with the magnificent 4–0 win over Newcastle in the Charity Shield. However, our coach, Brian Kidd, ever the cheerful one, was keen to stress we should not take the ease of our victory as an indication of how this season was going to proceed. Though we played some exciting and fluent football and clearly outplayed our opponents on the day, Kiddo was inclined to attribute our success to our being further advanced in our fitness programme than Newcastle.

The match was given enormous significance because of Newcastle's signing of a player who over the summer was confidently expected to be on his way to Old Trafford. As far as Alan Shearer is concerned, the story is a very simple one. Blackburn Rovers wouldn't sell him to us. If he had joined United he would have done well here, of that there is little doubt. The club made the utmost effort to get him to sign and offered him a fantastic amount of money. I suppose Jack Walker believed a transfer to Newcastle would be less of a blow to Rovers' fans. Blackburn are the only team not from a major city to have won the League in recent years. Their supporters may consider their club a rival of United, but United fans don't reciprocate. For them, Blackburn will always be a small team in the shadow of the really big Northern clubs.

Kiddo's sobriety about the new season appeared excessive after we seemed to carry on where we left off last May. It's time opinions of Wimbledon were revised. Our visit to Selhurst Park on 17 August was billed as the opening match no team would want. It's true I suppose, in that if you don't play well against them they will seize the opportunity and upset you. But we didn't go into this match expecting a particularly rough game and we didn't get one. Wimbledon are prepared to play football and we have done well against them in the past. We bring our own support, up to 17,000, so it's like playing at home.

I enjoyed watching this match from my position on the bench. Now that five substitutes can be named instead of three, I have more chance of getting on, though the bench needs to be big enough to take us all. When I finally made my entrance twelve minutes from time United were 2–0 up after goals by Eric and Denis, and all that was necessary was to keep the ball for the short period which remained. David Beckham hadn't picked up on this and he miss-hit a cross from 50 yards and scored a third. Somehow I think we'll be still seeing this goal next May. It has already been christened Goal of the Season, even by our usually cautious manager.

The Everton match at Old Trafford four days later was a very different game from the stroll around Selhurst Park, and in many ways it injected a much-needed note of reality into our defence of the Premiership. Everton's defeat of Newcastle showed us that they had begun the season in top form. The result was a triumph for our team talk in one respect, though I doubt the manager would see it in that way. We had discussed how they were going to play and what they were going to do and we were right: they did exactly what we predicted and scored two goals. What we missed from the manager's instructions was how we were supposed to stop it. For the first goal, Andrei Kanchelskis was allowed to bring down the ball and Duncan Ferguson turned brilliantly to score. For the second, Peter Schmeichel missed the cross, but we didn't cover the set pieces and corners which we we knew were going to be dangerous given Hinchcliffe's ability to deliver superb crosses and Ferguson's power in the air.

Watching from the sidelines once again was extremely frustrating because it was so easy to see what the problem was. Everton played five in the midfield and worked very hard to win the ball. Karel Poborsky, another new signing, was making his home debut and was finding it impossible to make any impact. Having said all this, we created plenty of chances which we failed to convert.

The Gaffer's answer was to put another (mature) body in midfield, so I came on. At half time, his instructions were to make sure the easy possession their midfielders had enjoyed became more difficult. This was not delivered to the accompaniment of smashing teacups (we have paper cups in the dressing room now anyway), but against a background of general disappointment and the belief that we could come back in the game – especially as we knew Everton would tire. We pulled the score level in the second half after a powerful header from Jordi Cruyff. The equalizer came from an own goal by Unsworth, who put the ball in the Everton net in sheer terror at seeing me bearing down on the ball.

Much was said beforehand about the hostile reception Andrei would meet on his return to Old Trafford. Though the crowd's disappointment was only natural, and it stands to reason that many can't understand why someone should want to leave this club, I think the way it has been reported made his departure appear more of a betrayal than it actually was. I don't think we'll ever know the full story of why he decided to go, even if it's only because so much gets lost in translation. I roomed with him for three years and I don't understand his reasoning. From a footballer's perspective you could say it was his choice, but we all tried to persuade him to stay. I graphically remember saying to him, "Andrei, what do you think you are doing?" Then again, I suppose I'm the last person to understand why he might want to go.

But the headlines the day after the game were all made by the Gaffer. I didn't know about his little two-step with Brian Kidd out on the pitch at the end of the match until I read the morning's papers. The Boss's protest was about time added on: he thought the referee hadn't played enough. He felt that Joe Royle was pressuring the official to bring the match to a premature close by waving his watch at him from the touchline – though I guess many people would suggest that we've done very well here from injury time in the past.

I played for the whole game against Blackburn on 25 August, let in two goals and got booked, but I was reasonably satisfied with my performance. My family all came to watch and it made me feel rather proud, though Siobhan and Laura (ten and seven years old respectively) found the first half enough and wanted to stay in the crèche for the second, where they could watch videos and play with the other children. Liam (our five-year-old) did me the favour of sticking the whole match out.

Roy Keane had gone in for an ankle operation and Nicky Butt hadn't recovered from a dead leg, so the midfield had to be completely reorganized. Ronny Johnsen started as a midfielder in Norway but for the last few years he has been a centre back, and he did very well considering this. Blackburn gave us a hard game. Our own performance ebbed and flowed. We started quite brightly, then they put on a great deal of pressure and we couldn't manage to clear the ball properly. For all that, we created plenty of chances and Eric Cantona could have given us an early lead.

I couldn't believe I was booked, and so early on in the game, for supposedly bringing Colin Hendry down. I'm hardly renowned for my strong tackling. I went for the ball and Hendry got there before me. I found out afterwards that it was the referee's first game in the Premier League. Though he performed creditably over the whole of the game, I think it was understandable that he wanted to assert his authority early on, but not that it had to be me. I remember thinking that this could be my first red card. It only takes one slip nowadays and a second decision goes against you. You go for the ball and you're off.

Though the score was the same, the game was very different from the previous week's draw against Everton. We could have won against Rovers, but Tim Flowers made some excellent saves to prevent us finding the winning goal. We have been punished for all our mistakes. The first goal Blackburn scored was partly my fault: I let Kevin Gallagher run off unmarked on to a cross. Jordi made the scores level five minutes later. For the second, Bohinen turned me on the edge of the box and the ball came off Denis Irwin's studs and was deflected into the net.

Our team is effectively quite different from last season and the new personnel will take some settling in. Ole Gunnar Solskjaer hasn't required much time to do that, however. He wants to shoot from everywhere and has a good eye for goal – fortunately for us, in this match.

Yesterday I enjoyed the rain like everyone else on the August Bank Holiday. Maureen, my wife, and I decided that we wouldn't take our three children on any special outing. Our last trip, to the Camelot theme park, embarrassed them horribly as I became another one of the attractions on view.

Today I went back to Old Trafford where I spoke to the Chairman, Martin Edwards, about the new contracts being negotiated by Nicky Butt and Paul Scholes. I felt quite privileged to be asked by both my team mates to sit in on the discussions; I was briefly involved when they signed their contracts last year. Both players had a very good idea of what they were looking for, but my presence made them feel more comfortable; going to see the Chairman and the specific language of the negotiations can be intimidating. I just sat and listened and pointed out one or two things, before going away with the figures to check they all added up. Nicky and Paul were happy and will probably sign tomorrow.

Of course, some players would have agents to do this job for them. There's no doubt that young players who are on the edge of the England team will soon have plenty of opportunities to make money in various ways both in and outside football. These attractions will crop up in another year's time and they'll sign new contracts. Each one of the young stars here is in a position to consolidate himself financially for the rest of his life. They may not have agents, but they do have accountants and have already bought themselves houses. They've all got lucrative boot contracts which pay very, very good money and they don't really need to get involved in any other commercial schemes. If anyone does have a proposal for a player, they should approach them directly, rather than having someone (such as an agent) going out doorstepping on the player's behalf. At the moment Nicky, Paul and the others need to concentrate on promoting their football careers.

There is now such a huge number of ways footballers can make money, especially if they play for Manchester United. People are falling over themselves to represent them. Ryan Giggs is an example of how a player's outside projects can be handled well. Through his agent, two or three things are arranged every year; these projects are kept to a minimum, so that they don't interfere with his football. That way, the hundreds of people who want to pitch him an idea don't overwhelm him. It's important to the manager that Manchester United should be Ryan's main priority, but that doesn't mean Ryan will necessarily miss out on worthwhile money-making opportunities. It's obvious that the best way any footballer can maximise his earning potential, as the business people say, is to play his best football in a successful and glamorous team.

Today's training was a change. We were able to play an eleven-a-side match as our numbers were depleted because of international duties. The

Gaffer has expressed some concern that David Beckham's call-up for England may have come too soon, but I think it will do him good. Every-one wants to play for their country, whether they are seventeen or thirty one (like Colin Hendry). I played for Scotland when they qualified for the World Cup in Italy. I wasn't actually chosen for the squad which went to the finals, though I believe I should have been. The high point of my international involvement was the European Championship in 1992. The team played such good football against the Dutch, the Germans and the CIS, beating the CIS in the match to decide third place, and finally I scored my first goal for Scotland. A record of thirty caps and two goals has a certain symmetry to it – though I feel I must point out in my own defence that those were not thirty full games by any means. And now my children believe they are English. Convincing them otherwise is going to be a long job.

The big news of the day was the European draw. We knew we were going to get either Juventus or Milan, and were reasonably happy with Juve. I'm looking forward to going to Turkey for the Fenerbahçe game: there is always plenty of atmosphere in front of a Turkish crowd. Seeing Rapid Vienna's name reminds me of an unpleasant ninety minutes when I played against them for Celtic in 1984 at Parkhead. One of their players was allegedly struck by a missile from the crowd and came out after half-time with his head swathed in bandages. He looked like Tutankhamun. I was very near the incident and something was thrown on the pitch, but I am sure that it didn't inflict enough damage to require mummification. UEFA ordained a replay, which had to take place more than 150 miles from Glasgow; the "neutral" ground chosen was Old Trafford.

Inconsistency continued to be the theme of our next two performances. At the Baseball Ground on 4 September, we played three across the back, a tactic which was supposed to be a preparation for the European game. It was reasonably successful, in that we created a lot of chances in the first half, but we failed to score. Derby scored from a free kick, and they shouldn't have done. We only had two men in the wall instead of three. I don't know whose responsibility that was, but it shouldn't have happened. David Beckham equalized with a great shot in the second half, but Derby changed their formation at half time and we found it hard to create the same openings as before.

In the Leeds away match on the following Saturday, we suddenly seemed to find the spark that we had been missing. I've certainly experienced the hostile atmosphere at Elland Road many times, but when I'm out on the pitch it never intimidates me. I enjoy it. The time you really are aware of it is when you arrive at the ground and get off the coach. There's always a big, vocal crowd and plenty of abuse. I just find it gives things an edge.

As for the match itself, we had a dream start and quite honestly the 4–0 scoreline didn't do us justice. Fluency and speed, the main features of our play when we are at our best, were in evidence throughout. Our fans were particularly supportive. This time we took three or four thousand, in contrast to the much smaller number last year, and they were all behind the goal making plenty of noise. Sitting on the bench again, as I was for most of the match, I could really appreciate the crowd. I don't know how it is that one person can think of something funny on the spur of the moment and communicate it to the whole crowd so it acts as one, but at one point they all went "Sshush" with their fingers on their lips at the Leeds fans, who had gone decidedly quiet. I enjoyed that.

I also had the privilege of watching Eric miss a penalty. We'd been saying for some time that he was due a miss, and though the goalkeeper dived the wrong way, the ball slipped by the wrong side of the post. As for him taunting the fans when he scored, as was later claimed, wasn't it just that he lifted his arms in a Gallic shrug? I can understand the way the Leeds fans react as they do towards him. It is the biggest possible compliment, because it shows how much they really adored him before he left for Old Trafford – and still do, secretly.

There is a fine line between player behaviour which is deemed to be inciting trouble in the crowd and that which is just an expression of joy or frustration during a game. It's the same thing with swearing and shouting out on the pitch. It's not so much what you say, more how you say it and where it is directed. You can't get away from the fact that some things you do will stir up spectators. Certainly the police have spoken to the club about how players could and should be more careful – not in any aggressive way, you understand, but to remind us that we have a certain responsibility. Still, things have changed. I remember when fans regularly ran out on to the pitch, without any incitement, because it was the thing to do. I will, of course, be forever remembered for one spectacular moment of indiscipline against Arsenal in the 1990/91 season, when I was one of several players involved in an on-pitch brawl. I wish it had never happened, and I don't have to think very hard when interviewers ask me to nominate my worst moment in football. I am also condemned to relive it constantly, as whenever there is an article or feature about the misdemeanours of footballers it is always accompanied by a large photo of the "pitched battle". I'm right in the middle with a strange expression on my face. The incident has been given another lease of life, given media interest in the trend of "New Laddism".

The fracas at Old Trafford was really just an accident. I tangled with Nigel Winterburn, and all hell broke loose and everyone else started getting involved, including normally quiet types like Mark Hughes, Paul Ince and Denis Irwin. Within a few minutes, the red mist had cleared and I was looking around in disbelief. I couldn't believe I'd just done what I had in fact just done. The referee came towards me and I thought, "I've got to be sent off here. I've never been sent off in my life but I'll just have to go off here. The referee can't do anything else. Violent conduct, and I'll deserve it." But I wasn't even booked. Not that I thought I'd got away with anything, because I knew the real trouble would start once the match was over. I was fined two weeks' wages and that cured me forever.

The worst thing of all was watching myself on television behaving very badly. My perceptions had been so distorted by rage that I hadn't actually remembered what had happened accurately. I was convinced I'd only kicked Nigel once, but that wasn't the case at all. Archie Knox, the coach, could hardly contain his laughter when he watched with me. "What the **** came over you?" he managed to gasp out when not rendered speechless with laughter. I couldn't tell him, because I honestly didn't know myself.

This week, we had training on the Sunday after the Leeds match, as we always do before a European game, and there was a great deal of running. We knew it was going to happen, but I could really have done without it. I remember thinking, "This is going to make me feel bad for the rest of the day," and I'd only played for 15 minutes at the end of the Elland Road tie the previous day. Yes, we did benefit from the training session, but when your chest is hurting and your lungs are burning, the beneficial side isn't exactly uppermost in your mind. I thought I'd be falling asleep on the sofa and grumpy with the kids who were getting ready for their first day back at school tomorrow. I surprised myself by feeling quite good and I enjoyed being with them, despite the fact that my five year old, Liam, refused to go to bed before ten.

2

Turin casts a shroud

"Come on now, that's really childish, stop that!"

We flew out to Turin on the Tuesday (the Juventus match was on the Wednesday) at about eight in the morning, which was very early indeed for some of our party. Despite the fact that this should probably be the last club to economize on air travel, United had chartered a plane from a French company, described in the Guardian as a "shoestring operation" whose fleet consisted of three ancient Boeings. The planes looked all right to me, though the service was slightly odd. Normally you get asked if you want a drink virtually as soon as you are in the air but no one came round for ages. This probably explains why the press may not have been entirely comfortable with the arrangements. The food, drinks, everything arrived at once after about an hour. The landing was perfectly fine. There was quite a thud, but at least we got down in one piece. I was reassuring one of the travellers who was nervous about flying by discussing chaos theory. "A crash like that can't happen to the same club twice," I ventured. "I mean, it just can't happen that the plane would plummet down like that a second time." Strangely, even this observation failed to calm him.

I was really enthusiastic to see the Fiat factory in Turin, which apparently was built with a test track on the roof. I was trying to persuade one of the pressmen, Rob McCaffrey I think it was, that it would be a fantastic spot for an interview. He was unconvinced, which turned out to be a good thing because it had been demolished anyway. We had a meal at the hotel, the footballers' staple – pasta. I think they must have flown the sauces in from somewhere where they can't make pasta sauces, like Australia, because they were awful. We travel to a country with some of the best food in the world and have a terrible meal. Perhaps the hotel had been instructed by the club to make the food as unappetising as possible to stop us overeating. Then we went to our rooms and I listened to Karel Poborsky's mobile phone ringing for a few hours.

It actually took thirty-five minutes to get from the hotel to the Stadio delle Alpi. We had a police escort and the way that the Italian drivers took absolutely no notice of it was particularly endearing. The convoy was supposed to be carving a way for us through the traffic. One woman police officer stuck a very small contraption, like a lollipop with a light at the end, out of the back window. Italian motorists would need to have very good eyesight to see it. They ignored it completely.

Compared with the Stadio delle Alpi, Old Trafford is the height of luxury. I had a look at the seats where our fans were to sit and they were pieces of plastic set into concrete steps. These foreign stadia often appear magnificent from the outside but on closer inspection they have some pretty basic features missing – like no toilet seats in the away dressing room, a special feature of the "palatial" San Siro. And as for the game, we lost 1–0. Well, what can you say? We had our tactics worked out, we knew how we should be playing, but in the end we just couldn't seem to play. Yes, we know that they have some good players, that they work hard, but we can do all those things too and it didn't go for us. I think much has been said to build up Italian football, to overhype it. We have the same level of skill and their football was very direct. I was on the bench when the first goal they scored was disallowed and I saw the linesman's flag go up straight away. I must have been the only person in the stadium who wasn't getting excited. Technically, I suppose it was offside...

We did improve in the second half. I came on as part of a reorganization. As I said before, you can arrange your tactics beforehand and you can tell players how and where you want them to play but they may not be able to or won't put that into practice. Despite our better shape we had only one clear chance in the form of Karel's header. Someone suggested he might have scored if his hair had been a few feet shorter.

Afterwards we were really quiet. As the evening was very warm we sat outside for a time, cooling off. It was a relief of sorts to be in the semi-darkness where we could all keep our own counsel. In the dressing room afterwards there had been nothing to say. We were just very disappointed that we hadn't been able to play as we know we can. The manager came in to speak to us afterwards but we had to wait a while for him to be interviewed by the press. That was unusual, because he normally comes in to speak to us first; it is a rule that whatever happens we meet together to talk briefly about it.

Defeat used to stay with me for a very long time, but it's just not as bad these days. I'm more philosophical now; I don't go home and kick the cat and shout at the kids. I kept thinking how ironic it was that if we still had the two-leg, aggregate system of old we'd be really pleased to have lost 1–0, to have kept the scoreline to that in Turin. I did honestly believe that we could get something out of the match, a draw or maybe better. I suppose part of the reason for my high expectations is that Manchester United lose so few games. We're a team that just doesn't expect to lose: we all believe that we can just go out and win the next match and do something positive about it.

No defeat will ever compare with the time Leeds pipped us to the Championship. I carried that with me the whole summer. I kept reliving it and people asked me about it over and over again. But the lesson we learnt was so valuable. I couldn't wait for the new season to start as I was completely determined to win the Championship the next year. In Turin, even though our game wasn't going well I loved every minute of it and it was a great pleasure to play.

On the way back to England, everything went smoothly. The travel arrangements were highly organized. Usually when we arrive at an airport, we have to wait for the media who are filing their copy, but this time it didn't seem to take them very long. When we flew back to Manchester, landing safely with another thud, there was someone from GMTV at the airport. When we spotted him, we all groaned, as it was the last thing we needed. It was very funny, because the man they sent was softly spoken and timid, quite a pleasant person really. He stuck a microphone in front of Andy Cole and asked him ever so politely to say something. Andy walked straight past him. I had to make a real effort not to laugh out loud at his crestfallen expression. The sight of me grinning after a 1–0 reverse wouldn't have made a very good impression, so I stalked past grim-faced like the rest. It never bothers me seeing the press – we've all got our jobs to do. I was home by one o'clock.

We returned to find the papers fussing about women becoming referees, with the appearance of Wendy Toms, the first woman to qualify as a League referee. I don't see any reason against it. Women are more perceptive and observant, they notice things more. As for fears that women officials won't be able to stamp their authority on the game, whoever said that can't be married to one. I wouldn't feel the slightest bit uncomfortable at being refereed by a woman, and if some other players might, that's their problem. If women have the training to do the job then they shouldn't be prevented by those sort of objections.

Our next match was the League game against Forest at Old Trafford.

We started off making life difficult for ourselves by giving away an early goal. After that, we played fluently and there was an impressive rhythm and style to our play. It soon became apparent that it wouldn't be much of a problem for us to win this match, but we needed the first goal. When we scored two just before half-time we knew we wouldn't lose. It was an ideal time for Ryan to score with a header for the second, but the first goal was an interesting one because it took a very rare mistake by Stuart Pearce to let in Solskjaer. I came on for Nicky Butt in the forty-first minute when he picked up a calf injury. Norman Fox in the Independent on Sunday commented the next day that "the replacement of Butt by Brian McClair shortly before half-time added some powerful midfield thrust", though gentle midfield nudge would have been a bit more accurate. Fifty minutes was a good run out for me. I can just about last that long now. We played equally well in the second half but didn't convert the possession into goals, until two late ones from Eric. We could have won with a much bigger scoreline than the 4–1 result.

Butt's return to fitness saw me warming the bench for the full ninety minutes at Villa Park the following Saturday. Games against Villa have always been hard for us. We still remember the defeat at the start of last season, though the score in that game didn't reflect our second half performance when we could have scored two or three. Overall this time we should have won the game, even though Villa have strengthened their squad and been among the front runners. They hardly created a goal-scoring opportunity. Raimond van der Gouw stood in for Peter, who was ill, and he didn't have a save to make. We had the best chances. Giggs hit the post and Andy Cole who came on at half-time hit the bar with a header. After that it fizzled out to a boring 0–0 draw. I know that beforehand we would have settled for that result away to Villa, but we should have won. It wasn't that they were unambitious, but we defended well and had excellent possession.

Just four days later, our campaign to progress to the knock-out stage of the Champions' League resumed when we met SK Vienna at Old Trafford on 25 September. An UEFA ruling meant that I watched this one not even from the bench but from the lofty heights of the directors' box, along with Angus Deayton and Frank Skinner. Frank Skinner looked terrible. I wonder if he keeps an extra head somewhere which he puts on for his TV appearances. Angus Deayton travelled to the game in a ridiculously long stretch limo which was later seen trying to make a U-turn on Chester Road, to the accompaniment of much vocal encouragement from passing supporters and other road users.

The team was so aware of how important the first European game here was. The home games are the ones you have to win – experience has taught us that if nothing else. We had such an excellent start to the game; the tempo of our play was particularly pleasing. We hoped to get an early goal and, though that didn't happen despite our pressure, we did get two goals close together in the first half from Ole, who has exceeded all expectations with his early successes, and David Beckham. They effectively put an end to the tie. I thought we could get four or five, but it seemed difficult to keep up the momentum.

In the second half Vienna did a little bit better, because in all frankness they didn't play very well and their poor performance was a surprise. We'd had reports from their game against Fenerbahçe in which they were the better team, though the word was that they were capable rather than anything special. Juventus's victory in Istanbul was also a bonus. I suppose the TV evidence afterwards suggested Vienna could have had a penalty and we were maybe a bit fortunate. The crowd went loopy at the end, Mexican waves and singing their heads off. They performed "Down by the Riverside" and "Cheer up, Kevin Keegan" among other, older favourites. I think it was partly because the game had got so boring! It really was quite weird how they almost seemed to lose all sense of what was going on on the pitch. Vienna could have pulled one back in the last ten minutes but no one appeared to give it much heed. But the atmosphere was electric and the team did appreciate that it was nearly a sell-out, given that it was mid-week, a 7.30 pm kick-off and broadcast live on TV. There was huge excitement and I think it was apparent that it gave the team a positive feeling about the game from the beginning. The fans obviously want us to do well in Europe, especially after the disappointment of Turin and the negative comments which followed it in the newspapers. So many people are waiting for us to fail. It's an enormous compliment, when you think of it.

I don't like the idea of having two English teams in the Champions' League next year. The decision hasn't been made for football reasons but rather to please the television companies in the so-called eight strongest football nations. No team is going to turn it down, are they? Certainly Manchester United won't, if they need the new rule to get through. But it's not in the spirit of football. In a way, it's a potential nightmare for the second club, who will have to start the season two weeks earlier to get through the qualifying rounds (though Kiddo would be delighted by that). If the club also has international players, along with the schedule for World Cup qualifying matches their close season might disappear. There must be some games in June. We'll just have to win the Premiership again – or the Champions' League. It's worth the extra effort to keep those two weeks off.

We had a four week break before we were in European action again in Istanbul, the scene of some interesting ties in the past. The plan was to fly out to Turkey on Monday 14 October for Wednesday's tie with Fenerbahçe, as we've found from experience that when the flight is longer we need the extra day. Last time we were in Istanbul the hotel had a magnificent view over the Bosphorus. It had a shoeshine service for about ten pence which pleased the directors enormously. They're thinking of installing something similar at Old Trafford.

We arrived at Manchester airport at midday. It looked as though it was all going to be very comfortable as we had a little lounge to sit in, but then we discovered that our plane was still in Tenerife. We were offered some sandwiches, but because I am picky I couldn't eat them – I prefer them made with dry bread. The thought of margarine or butter makes me sick, probably because I have some sort of allergy to them, like I do to house dust. Not that this ever gets me off the vacuuming at home. By the time the plane arrived I was starving and had to pay for my earlier fastidiousness by tucking into the beef stew, so I'll know for a certainty where I caught it.

We arrived at Istanbul airport at 8 pm and it was very quiet indeed. There were no hordes of demonstrating Turkish supporters like the last time I came here for the Galatasary tie, just crowds of press men looking for them. On Tuesday we watched a video of Fenerbahçe against Juventus and went to the stadium to train. While we were there we were joined by Bobby Charlton. Afterwards he told me how much he still missed playing and it was quite obvious from the enthusiasm he displayed running about and joining in the exercises and little games. Eric nutmegged him and he wasn't too happy about it.

Turin casts a shroud

On Wednesday we went for a walk with an armed guard, who followed us with guns at the ready. Nobody would stand next to Peter, since he was supposed to have offended the whole of the Turkish nation the last time Galatasary played at Old Trafford by throwing a Turkish pitch-invader off the pitch. Then followed the team talk, during which the manager named the team (I was to be on the bench) and we watched some more video footage of our opponents. I read the local English-language newspaper, the *Turkish Daily News*, which said that any halfwit could work out how to beat Fenerbahçe. It also warned people to stay off their balconies if either Fenerbahçe or Galatasary won tonight, as the last time this happened supporters fired pistols into the air in celebration and people were killed as they looked over their balconies or were caught by the ricochets.

Those of a suspicious mind may have worried when the coach that was to drive us to the stadium turned out to be decidedly shabby and different from the one which brought us from the airport to the hotel. The other coach could not be insured for our journey.

Fenerbahçe are supposed to have between eighteen and twenty-eight million supporters in Turkey, but there were only 28,000 in the stadium. They were in good voice, though they did have a little help. The public address interrupted the first twenty minutes of the game and it was ear-splitting. From where I was on the sidelines I could hardly bear it. None of the English speakers knew what the announcer was saying, but Bobby Charlton got up a few times and shouted down to the UEFA official to ask him what he was doing about it. At one point Sir Bobby appeared to be jumping up and down. The Estonian-quality floodlights were turned down at the start so that the flares and flaming paper lit by the crowd could be seen to best effect and the smell of burning cordite and the swirling white smoke filled the stadium. I had the unenviable job of passing on a UEFA dictate to Peter that his towels should be removed from the goal. He advised me in turn to remove myself from the pitch in his customary understated style, or so I presume, having only caught the word "off" as the public address blared out again. Out on the pitch we managed to get ourselves into the game more and more after an shaky first twenty minutes. The two goals from Beckham and Cantona, coming as they did at the beginning of the second half within two minutes of each other, killed the tie off. We were thrilled to win away at last in Europe.

Despite the relatively low-key reception we received in Turkey, the papers were not going to be cheated of their "Turkish Hell" headlines. According to the stories they ran, Paul Scholes and the Nevilles were showered with glass as our coach was bombarded and their lives put at risk. In fact, literally seconds before the coach was hit, Brian Kidd battered the window as a joke and we were all laughing. I was reading and looked up and saw out of the corner of my eye a brick lobbing towards us as if in slow motion. It hit the window but just knocked through tiny bits of glass, like powder. Apparently Sir Bobby was busy admonishing Kiddo for what he thought was more of his horseplay, saying, "Come on now, that's really childish, stop that!" We were all really unmoved, but we did put the lights out to make the coach less of a target. Similar situations must have happened many times to other teams. What did bother us was being phoned up early next morning after arriving home at 4.30 am by journalists anxious for a story.

3
Off the pitch

"Does Eric recite poetry in the dressing room?"

Sunday was a free day and, as part of my benefit year, we held a lunch for supporters. It was just an idea we decided to try out and we were pleased by its success. We had a hundred or so people in for a little food and a raffle at Old Trafford. Gary and Phil Neville came along and there was a question and answer session. I don't think I was very good, in that my brain refused to work halfway through. Jim Ryan was saying that I seemed to spend all my time not giving an answer. The supporters would ask questions like "What's your favourite whatever... ?" and I'd say, "I don't have a favourite goal/ground/game" or "It wouldn't be fair to the digestive biscuit to say that the rich tea was the best." As Jim said, if I had been asked what my favourite colour was I would have said black because it's not a colour, or white, because it's a mixture of all the colours. I was asked who was my favourite player and I couldn't think of one, not one. I couldn't even think of Pelé – and that would have been true, as I idolised him when I was a kid and I'm still convinced that the goal Gordon Banks was supposed to have saved went in.

Maybe I thought they'd ask me something different, but I suppose they are the sort of questions fans always want to ask. It's like when the Gaffer says at the end of his team talk, "Has anybody got any questions?" and there's never anything. Once I said, "Yes, I've got a question." The Gaffer was very pleased until I added, "Where do babies come from?" I've never tried that one again. The temptation to do something like that is always there. The other day I was watching him while he was giving his talk and he was doing this little dance, and I thought I'd ask him what he was doing. But sometimes he just doesn't get it and neither does anyone else and it's just embarrassing. So I waited and asked him afterwards, "What was that dance you were doing? I thought it might be a waltz but couldn't be sure." He waved me away muttering darkly under his breath. He's ticked me off twice for inattention this season, but I'm the only one who does listen. I've told him I could go back through the entire team talk and repeat it word for word.

The team talk is very important for our manager. He seems, however, to have a growing oversensitivity about the risk of repeating himself, so he keeps it short. Andy Roxburgh as Scotland manager always had a lot of video tape featuring spliced-together action of our opponents. You can give out too much information and players just stop listening as they can't assimilate it all, but some managers say nothing whatsoever.

On the following Monday there was another benefit event, a boxing evening. I'm not the world's biggest boxing fan, but for my testimonial it was a fairly easy thing for the committee to organize. We had a black-tie dinner followed by the bouts. There was a good turn out from my team mates, but surprisingly the Neville brothers failed to arrive. Next day we discovered they went to the wrong hotel. Unfortunately, this evening set up a conflict for me: the opening of the Red Café, a new restaurant at Old Trafford, planned for Wednesday had meant that a reserve fixture was rescheduled for this night. I don't feel comfortable not playing for them, especially when I was out instead making money for myself by watching men hitting each other. The evening had the time-honoured format. The manager led the toast to me, I said a few words and he did the same. And then on came Bernard Manning... Fortunately, he contented himself with slaughtering the Gaffer and Kiddo and completely ignored me. It was highly amusing. Brian Kidd went some way towards making himself a little happier by putting in a "pity bid" for my shirt, which was auctioned alongside those of Eric and Ryan.

The first bout of the boxing was very unfortunate. One of the men, who was having his first professional fight, was knocked unconscious.

The rest of the bouts were far more politically correct: they became a sort of protest against boxing as the fighters played at not hitting each other.

As heads were being pounded, I thought about the recent studies which show the effect on players' brains of heading the ball, hastening the onset of degenerative brain conditions and dementia. I often think about this in training, as the ball is winged in the air towards me. Another four or five headers and I'll know what it's like to be Nicky Butt. But it must be different for today's footballers; think of the players who are fifty or sixty now, and the weight of the leather balls they used to head in their day. I had one of those when I was young. You couldn't kick it, let alone head it.

Wednesday's opening of the Red Café at Old Trafford was the big social event of the week – or, to put it another way, everyone had to go. It's part of my unofficial duties at the club to liaise between players and the commercial operation and in this case I gave out the order to attend, though I was the least enthusiastic about it. I was getting ready at about quarter to seven when Maureen called out, "There's someone at the door for you." On the doorstep, with a Jaguar parked behind him, was a stranger. I stared at him and eventually he said, "I have got the right house, haven't I?"

"Pardon?" said I.

"McClair?" he went on, "I've come to pick you up. My orders are to take you to Old Trafford."

"Oh, no, no, no, you're all right, I'll just get myself there," I told him, and sent him away. Then he went across the road and picked up Gary Pallister. I drove to the ground, parked my car and was talking to a couple of security men who told me that there was a limo waiting to ferry people round to the front of the cafe when the Jag dropped them off. "Oh, right," I said, "Well, no, I don't think so." No way was I getting into a pink Cadillac convertible, so I walked round like I usually do. Music was blaring out and spotlights swept the sky. I didn't see it myself, but I think they also projected huge match pictures on the back of the North Stand.

I came up the side and got as far as the crush barriers erected to hold back the adoring crowds. Completing the film-premiere scenario, a woman who was acting as hostess announced into a mike, "And we've got another car coming. Who could this be?" I took the opportunity to nip in quickly before I could be seen and forced to say something. Nicky Butt came in about ten minutes later, red faced, and said, "That was just so embarrassing. I couldn't get the door handle open to get out of the car."

I stood by the door, chatting to Kiddo and the Gaffer and watched the celebrities arriving, among them Bill Wyman and Caroline Aherne. Up came a reporter from the *Daily Express* who asked, "Do you know that Eric hasn't come, but he's sent a poem instead?" He read it out to me and asked my opinion about it. I said it sounded fine to me. Then he asked, "Does Eric recite poetry in the dressing room?"

"Er, no," I replied. "Funnily enough he doesn't, no."

"Well," he went on, "Did you understand the remark he made about the seagulls?"

"Aye, yes," I said.

"Could you tell me what it means?"

"No," I told him. "You have to open up your mind to these things."

I could just imagine Eric standing up in the dressing room announcing, "I 'ave somethink to say. I 'ave a leetle poem for yew." I should have told the reporter that Eric does indeed do that regularly, and sometimes we're so moved we're all crying. I could have said that we've all started contributing our own verses and last week it was Scholesy's turn to open his heart. I think the reporter would have bought it. However, the manager was standing very close by.

These sort of evenings are now part and parcel of the footballer's life. It was a free night out, but I didn't stay long. I had a drink of water and nothing to eat. I suppose it would have been more fun if I could have sat down anonymously in the corner and watched it all – and maybe found someone to talk with who wasn't anything to do with football. But I wasn't in the mood for that. It felt very much like I was working rather than enjoying myself.

Off the pitch

On Thursday I flew to Cork, taking advantage of the international weekend, for one of my testimonial dinners and had the pleasure of reading a highly critical, but very well-written, article about it on the front page of the *Cork Examiner* on the journey home the next morning. Eric and David May kindly accompanied me to the event, which was for about 300 Irish supporters. When we were arranging it we emphasized that Eric wouldn't do anything with the press or take part in formal question and answer sessions. But it's impossible to tell them.

It went very well, except that there were fans all over the place. News of our visit had spread rapidly so there were hundreds at the airport and the hotel. At the dinner itself, we were making sure that everyone got autographs and it was mayhem at one point as the participants wouldn't stay at their tables and wait for us to move around. I think by the close everyone was happy, but we didn't finish until after midnight. The *Cork Examiner* was unhappy that Eric would only say "no" or "non", missing the point that he was there to keep 300 people content and he more than did that. There was an auction for his strip, and a huge fan of Eric was desperately bidding for it. In the end Eric bid for it himself and gave it to the guy. He bought his own strip with his own money and gave it away. The man was a real fan of Eric, with a tattoo of him on his shoulder. I expect he'll be an even bigger fan now.

In the paper, the journalist quoted the sum I was supposed to have made from the event. It was way above what I expected. When I read it I said to Chris, my friend who is head of the committee organizing the year, "Chris, is there anything you want to tell me about this?" The article was part of the general line about Manchester United, pointing out that McClair was coming over to Ireland, lining his pockets, then citing the example of an Irish player who had come upon hard times. It went on to ask if it was a reflection on Irish fans that they cared more for English teams than their own. It's fair comment in a way. Testimonials are contentious and their rationale questioned in some quarters. Obviously, I can see the point of them and want to profit from the year as best I can. However, I do think that the amount of attention we got was because Eric was there. If it had just been David May and I, it wouldn't have excited any comment. I was very conscious all the time that we had to look after Eric. He was doing me a very big favour as the adulation he receives is enormous, but also so stifling and often overwhelming. The next day the Gaffer questioned me very closely about the evening. If anything had gone amiss with Eric I would have had some explaining to do.

The idea behind everything we've organized is that I want to give something back to people who support the testimonial. I want them to come and feel that they've had some value and a good time. But of course we are going to make money from it; that's what it's for.

At the airport for the return journey they kept the plane back for fifteen minutes for us as we were late. We were running for it when the officials said, "Don't worry about that, just sign this for us, will you, and while we're at it we'll have a few photographs." It reminded me of the time last year we went over to Limerick for a supporters' club event. We were picked up at the airport and the coach stopped at a bar and the organizers said, "We'll just have one in here before we go on", and we did and signed autographs for whoever was inside. Then we had to go and pick up Denis who was with the Republic squad, but before then we just "had to nip in to this bar to see so-and-so" with similar results. As we picked up Denis we "just dropped into" another place. It was quite a big pub, and there were three people inside when we arrived. Five minutes later there were forty. I said to someone, "How did you know we were going to be here?" "To be sure," he replied, "It says it here," and he had a programme which marked every time and pub we just happened to be passing!

So far this season I have only started one first-team match, so my main contribution has been in the Pontin's League. The Reserves have had patchy form of late. Against Tranmere in September we won 5–0. I scored, though the game was spoiled rather when their centre half was injured and had to go off. Tranmere had to change it around and lost their momentum. I've already achieved my goal target for the Reserves this season: one. I was trying to keep up with Terry Cooke and he eventually, for a change, cut it back in my direction and I put a nice strike into the corner. However, we also played at Sheffield Wednesday and lost 2–1. We should have done better, though we retrieved the situation somewhat by putting in one of our best performances at Anfield on 5 October.

We kicked off at three o'clock, a different experience from the usual for the Reserves, as we were playing on a Saturday made free by the international weekend. There was quite a good crowd too, of about 10,000, and playing in front of a crowd like that at Anfield must be worthwhile for a professional. Even more satisfying was that we played stylishly and won 3–0 with some fluent football. But there was a really negative side to this match as Andy Cole was badly injured. No one realized how serious it was at the time. It was a bad challenge, although Neil Ruddock said he tried to play the ball. Andy went down very heavily. I knew he was going to hospital that night, but I thought it was merely a precaution. The next time I saw him he was in plaster and it transpires that he also had something cracked or heavily bruised in his other knee. He can get about on his crutches and therefore can still do some work in the gym but it may be December before he returns. It's so unfortunate for him after his pneumonia at the start of the season, and he had worked very hard indeed to regain his fitness from that. He'll have to do yet another bout of intense, pre-season type training.

The Reserves team manager is Jim Ryan, who takes all of them for training except those who are in the first-team squad. Brian Kidd takes the first team for training and, depending on what exercises he wants to do on any particular day, he could be in charge of between twelve and sixteen bodies. Jimmy's squad will be comprised of a mixture of senior players and the younger professionals, selected by the youth team coach. It's all very scientific. Jimmy has a famous biscuit tin lid with magnetic tags on it with everybody's names on, so he can work out who he's got and who he hasn't. Kiddo asks for players to make up the numbers and Jim moves the names around on his biscuit tin. Something usually goes wrong and he ends up with an odd number, when the object of the exercise is to end up with an even one.

Jim's group changes all the time. The youth team and first team squad are fairly stable, but the Reserves are in a constant state of flux. I am the oldest outfield player but fortunately Raimond van der Gouw, the second choice goalkeeper, is seven months older than I am. The knowledge that you are not the oldest player is very important. However, I'm the senior pro, and as such have the awesome responsibility of supposedly setting a good example. When I play for the Reserves, I want to play as well as I can. I feel the same wherever I play football. I would never want anyone to think that any game is beneath me, and playing is very enjoyable wherever you do it. In that way, I hope I am an example. With luck, all the Reserve team players will have careers in football; it's difficult enough getting there, but staying there is harder. You don't know who could be watching you in a game. And your reputation is important: you can spend ten years building up a decent name for yourself to see it disappear in one or two weeks.

United has an arrangement to play Reserves matches at Bury, designed to protect the pitch at Old Trafford. We have to play a certain number of Reserves games at Old Trafford to satisfy the regulations, and we try to play these at the beginning of the season when the grass can recover quickly. In mid-season, we play six games or so at Gigg Lane. It's so different. Bury is a great club, but the volume of games there means that their pitch suffers. They have first-team games and rugby league, and though the groundsman does a marvellous job he can't work miracles. It does become very, very sandy. But it's a stiff test, to go and try to play football on a far from perfect surface. It can only be good for the younger players. There are always scouts at our Reserve team games.

Family fun nights have done their bit to swell attendance for the Reserves at Old Trafford and elsewhere. Who could resist the combination of entry for £2, seeing the club mascot Fred the Red and having your face painted? Last year we went to Forest and there was a crowd of 15,000 for that kind of family event. It's not quite as busy on cold winter nights at Gigg Lane, where we have probably a couple of hundred spectators, but those who attend are among the most knowledgeable of our fans.

My other contribution to the development of the younger players is to point Ben Thornley towards his heritage. As he continues to recover from his horrific knee injury last year he still can't drive, so I've been picking him up. I discovered he has a Scots grandfather and passed this information on to the Scots cabal here. Jim Ryan and the Gaffer asked him what he'd do if he was phoned up and asked if he wanted to play for Scotland. We were all outraged by his passionless response.

"I'd have a better chance of playing for them, wouldn't I?" he mused.

"Forget it!" barked the Gaffer.

"Have you seen *Braveheart*? That's all you need to know," Jim Ryan informed him.

I tried to tempt him by describing a possible scenario where, in five years' time, Scotland are taking on England at Hampden Park or Wembley and the score is Scotland 2, England 0, courtesy of two own goals by Gary Neville (who currently goes out with Ben's sister, and by then might be his brother-in-law) from crosses from Thornley. His answer was merely that he hoped to find himself playing against me soon.

On the wall of the players' lounge are boards listing the United men who have represented the home nations internationally. It's a sign of the times and the changes in football that the last two names to represent Scotland are B J McClair and Jim Leighton. There can't have been many Manchester United teams with no current Scots internationals. There is such a good quality of life in Scotland and the profile of Scottish football has been rising, so perhaps there's no burning need for players to cross the border any more. On the other hand, there are those who say the quality of players being produced in Scotland is substandard. The favourite culprits for this are full-sized pitches for children's games, poor coaching, pushy parents and the better standard of living which blunts the hunger to succeed. You can do something about the first three, but it's not true that you can only be a great Scottish footballer if you've come straight out of the mines looking for a square meal. This old cliché is not a convincing argument for dismantling what remnants of the Welfare State the last seventeen years have left us.

Children have so many other things to occupy their time other than football nowadays. My mother, like every other professional footballer's mother, has said that I was completely obsessed with football; if I had a ball I didn't want to do anything else. But, then again, there was precious little else to do. When I was a boy, children's television consisted of *Play School* and *Blue Peter* (with *Magpie* as an alternative for the nonconformist). Now kids can watch programmes aimed at them all day. Liam loves to play football, but he also loves playing Nintendo.

When I was sixteen, I left school. I had taken my Highers, the Scottish equivalent of A levels, a year early, because of my December birthday. Mum and Dad always impressed on me the frailty of the human body when it is engaged in physical contact sports, so I was careful to make sure that I had these qualifications, despite the distractions of football. I followed the arche- typal football path of an apprentice, except that I had decided not to stay in Scotland. I travelled down to Aston Villa in 1980. Even then I wanted to continue with my education and take A-level Maths. This was all supposed to have been worked out for me by the Youth Development Officer at Villa Park. However, he left just as I arrived and his replacement didn't know anything about the arrangement and neither did Ron Saunders, the Villa manager. At that time, there was a feeling that too much education was bad for your legs or something. At Old Trafford nowadays, you have to go to college automatically as part of the YTS scheme that our young lads have enrolled on, and they take GNVQs. If any of the trainees are bright academically, there is a range of other courses they can take. John Curtis, for instance, is studying Economics at the moment. Older players can also continue with their education through the courses offered by the PFA – which are more geared towards football. The most familiar to the public is a physiotherapy course, organized to fit in with training, which can lead to a degree.

The year I spent over the border was very successful for Villa, because they won the Championship, but it didn't turn out as I expected. I had ended up there because I had been treated very well when I went down to the Midlands for a trial. I went to quite a few places, but Villa stood out for the care they took over potential apprentices. They gave the impression that they really wanted to sign me and would do the best they could for me in football. I think that this is one of the reasons United has been able to attract some of the best young talent at the moment, apart from the obvious allure of playing at such a famous club. Everyone, the Gaffer included, does their best to show prospective apprentices' parents that their sons' interests will be best served at Old Trafford. The manager always talks to parents personally and exercises that famous Gaelic charm.

During my year's apprenticeship, I grew and became a great deal fitter, even if my brain wasn't kept in shape. I was on a very steep learning curve. I scrubbed and cleaned boots in the time-honoured ritual. I mopped floors, cleaned the walls, picked up the dirty kit. I learned a lot... about cleaning! This part of an apprentice's training is supposed to instil humility, discipline and obedience. It was very difficult being away from home, but it gave me a certain independence, if nothing else. And I had the chance to play in a different environment. Having said all that, things didn't seem to be going anywhere and I decided that it would be best for my long-term future to return home to Scotland and go to university.

I'd been offered places at both Glasgow and Strathclyde. I can't rem-ember why I decided to go to university, but it certainly wasn't because I thought I didn't have a chance of eventually becoming a professional footballer. Youthful arrogance protected me from such worries. I knew I could go to university and play football part-time, and that's exactly what I did.

My degree course at Glasgow had Maths as its core, but I also studied the hard sciences of Physics and Chemistry. My original intention was only to combine two subjects, Physics and Maths, but I was interviewed by a Chemistry lecturer eager to drum up business. Three subjects were a bit much, especially after a year out during which my brain had been left on the sidelines. In my first lecture, which was Physics, I was completely left behind. "I'll never keep up with this!" I thought, but things did improve after that initial shock. Physics continued to cause me the biggest problem. I passed my first year exams in Maths and Chemistry (the Chemistry exam was, or so it appeared to me, easier than my Highers), but I couldn't get through the Physics paper. If I had passed all three subjects I would have been able to choose to specialise in two subjects in the second year, but because I hadn't I had to select an additional subject. I decided upon Statistics – a happy choice as I loved it. The Statistics lecturers were, for those days, very trendy, and invited you to call them by their first names, which impressed me no end at that age.

As important for me as being back studying was carrying on playing football. Davie Hay was assistant manager to Ally Macleod at Motherwell. A friend of mine, who was a scout for Motherwell, contacted Davie and told him I had come back from England. When I went to watch them play my home team, Airdrie, I was invited to go training with the Motherwell squad on Monday. I trained with them for all of two days, and on the third the manager called me into his office and asked me if I'd sign for them with a view to playing in the first team. I was flattered that they had been so impressed that they were prepared to give me a chance right away. However, I also contacted Celtic, as they had asked me to give them a call if things didn't work out in England. Celtic's chief scout told me that they wouldn't give me another trial and so I signed for Motherwell, which turned out to be a wonderful move. I spent two days a week training and the rest of the time at university. I enjoyed both enormously, but it was very hard balancing the demands of two opposing lifestyles.

I couldn't be a typical student and enjoy the student life, as I had to keep fit and make sure that I didn't fall behind in my work. I would have liked to have been a punk, but my parents would never have allowed it. Instead I compromised by wearing my Dad's duffel coat and my own sensible brogues – when I wasn't in my track suit. In the holidays I showed willing by making up any training that I might have missed. One big benefit about being a footballer and a student at the same time was that I always had a lot more money to spend than the other students.

When Davie Hay left Motherwell, planning to go to Florida, the ex-Rangers' manager, Jock Wallace, took over the club. I remember his first day in charge very well. It's always been part of Rangers' disciplinary code that players have to wear shirt, tie and smart trousers to training. You have to present yourself smartly turned out and shaved. As his introduction to the players, Jock took a pre-season training session. We were jogging around the pitch, warming up for training, when he shouted something at me at earsplitting volume. I couldn't understand a single word he was saying. I couldn't work out what he wanted, even when he continued to bellow at me, loud enough to shatter windows. It was at this point that Jock Wallace became convinced that I was sending him up by not doing what he had ordered, whatever that was. In truth, at the tender age of seventeen, I was terrified of him. I finally managed to decipher one word in the din, "Socks!", and the penny dropped. One of my tie-ups was loose, my sock had come down and it was causing him serious offence. He wanted me to jump to it and sort it out. It was hard to believe that all that fuss had been about such a trivial matter. I recall thinking, "We're not going to get on very well, here, are we?" I was right.

My development in football was in the hands of two disciplinarians and sticklers. Both Jock and Frank Connor had been NCOs in the army. They took turns in shouting at me to pull my socks up, literally and metaphorically, one relieving the other when exhaustion set in. The platitude I should spout here is that it was character forming, but at the time I resented it deeply. Looking back, I can see that this was a reflection of my own self pity, and that they were doing it for my benefit – though at the time I didn't see it like that at all. But this experience has not been wasted. Since then I've maintained their military standards, arriving for training and every club activity immaculately turned out.

Another glittering night. On Monday myself, David May, Raimond van der Gouw, Brian Kidd, Andy Cole and Phil Neville opened a new Hugo Boss store in Manchester. In the absence of the real stars, I got to hold the tape. Andy cut it and we all smiled and smiled. I was given a baseball cap, not an item of clothing I would wear from choice, with "Boss" emblazoned on it. I'll now have to get a job in management so I can wear it, because the Gaffer has forbidden it here. I shan't be changing my nickname or have "Boss" embroidered on my boots. I'm quite happy with Choccy (McClair as in eclair). It does have some wit and it's not just a boring extension of my name – Briany or McClairy. I have christened Karel Poborsky "Samson", but only I seem to like it. I was asked yesterday how long Karel would be allowed to keep his long hair. "As long as I can stand it," I quipped, as being his room mate does give me the opportunity to play Delilah. When Andrei Kanchelskis, my old room mate, annoyed me, I used to threaten to shave one of his eyebrows off when he was asleep. It was a real threat, given the coma-like state he frequently fell into. Oh, those long nights cooped up in hotels! The zany things we boys get up to!

As everyone else was on international duty, out of the country or injured, on 14 October myself, Paul Scholes and the Reserves made up the team for our unusual fixture at Bishop Auckland. The story is a romantic one, and I'm sure everyone knows it. Bishop Auckland have fallen into financial trouble, and this match was arranged to go a little way to repaying them for lending us players after the Munich air disaster by raising some money for them. When we got there, the ground was packed to its 4,000 capacity and one of the mascots who led us out was so overwhelmed by the occasion that he sobbed his heart out as we went on, while assuring me that he was having a wonderful time.

For the younger players it was also a very special night, but I'm not sure that tradition and history played such a big part in creating their state of mind as did the fact that McDonald's was sponsoring the game. They wouldn't normally be allowed this sort of food because of their training diets, but on such an occasion (and because we didn't wish to offend the sponsors) they could order what they liked. They really got stuck in. Still, their sense of responsibility didn't desert them entirely. Though the average order was a quarter pounder with cheese, medium fries and chicken McNuggets, it was generally washed down with Diet Coke. The sense of excitement when supplies were delivered to the team bus before we returned was enormous. I tucked into my plate of sandwiches and watched them eat: a visual demonstration of the generation gap.

As for the game, we scored after 30 seconds, but they played really well and worked hard and we couldn't score another goal in the first half. Eventually we won 4–1. The referee, George Courtney, was punctilious in playing the full 90 minutes. I played at right back for the last five and was eyeing the crowds of kids gathering on the sidelines. As the final whistle blew we sprinted for the dressing room with them in hot pursuit. I found myself locked out. It's my own fault, really; I'd locked everyone else out before the game.

As elder statesman, I did seven interviews that night. I haven't done as many for years. On our way back north we stopped at Scotch Corner, where I did a few minutes for the local TV and the BBC. At the ground, in a small room in the pavilion, there was a phone-in conducted by Malcolm Macdonald, aided by Malcolm Allison. The calls, which demonstrated the effect the Munich crash had on football fans of all teams, were very moving. Many older contributors recollected seeing the men playing who died in the disaster. I was made very uncomfortable, if not disorientated, by Malcolm Macdonald's idiosyncratic interviewing style. This consisted of allowing me to utter four or five words in answer before cutting in with a question or observation of his own. At one point I used the word mischievous, which prompted Malcolm to interject, "Mischievous! When have you heard a professional footballer say that word?" I didn't answer a single caller's question, but the programme was lively.

Before the game I also spoke to Sky Sports and Sky News, and found myself in the Tyne Tees radio car, on BBC local radio and elsewhere. I tried to keep saying something different to each but I ended up repeating myself constantly.

4
Chipped and battered

"We end up travelling by B roads
and up mountains."

Two League victories seemed to suggest that winter might see us hit top gear – as long as you didn't think too carefully about the actual performances. On 29 September, Jim Ryan, the Reserves' coach, and I watched the match at Old Trafford against Tottenham Hotspur. And what a boring game it was. We didn't play fluently at all, despite winning 2–0. Solskjaer's goal was interesting: the goalkeeper went down, missed the ball because of Ole's slip, and it went in. Last year when we played them, they made it hard and we snatched a win with Eric's late goal, but this year they really missed Armstrong's pace. David Howells was unlucky to be booked for hand ball. I agreed with the referee's decision to disallow the goal he scored, but it didn't look deliberate. I would have felt hard done by to be booked, but it's not easy for referees now every game is televised.

I don't see any way video playbacks and a third referee could be used in practise. Perhaps the only way a third official could be brought in is as an independent timekeeper. This would give the man in the middle some respite from being castigated by excitable Scottish managers for adding too much or too little extra time.

The major topic of discussion among the Scots at Old Trafford is our country's abortive tie in Estonia. It's difficult to see how the Estonia team just failed to turn up, though ironic that the UEFA official who checked out the stadium to ensure that it was fit for the game is Scottish. In fact, he's in charge of the programme to plan the way forward for Scottish football!

For the rest of the week, our preparation was focused on Saturday's Liverpool fixture, scheduled to kick off at 11.15 am, purely for the sake of live television. There were probably huge queues on the M6 at four in the morning as our travelling support pulled out all the stops again. We are supposed to eat at least three hours before a game, so this meant that breakfast was early. Instead of sleeping overnight in a hotel we were trusted to behave sensibly, get our own breakfasts and make our way to the ground on time. I reckoned we would win, as we are always at our best when we have to be for big games. Still, the last time we kicked off this early, we were 3–0 down after twenty minutes.

The unusual time for the kick-off gave an unreal air to the day. I arrived at Old Trafford at 9.15 am, but it was just as it always is nearly six hours later on a normal matchday, with crowds milling around outside. The team met to discuss how we were going to play against Liverpool, as their system is different from anyone else's. We had, of course, sorted this out a couple of days before the game, but we ran through it again to make sure that everyone was absolutely certain about what they had to do.

In the first half, all went according to plan and David Beckham scored our goal after a nicely worked move with Ole Gunnar Solskjaer. The scheme failed magnificently in the second half and Liverpool dominated. Only some great saves from Peter allowed us to emerge with three points.

Then it was back down to earth with a vengeance. On 20 October, in our next League match, we were beaten 5–0 at St James' Park. What am I supposed to say about this result? The words being bandied about are "blip" and "aberration". To be quite honest, we didn't even feel we played particularly badly. The first goal was down to poor defending. We had talked about people picking up opposing players in the box, and

Peacock was allowed a free header – not a particularly good header at that, but it was a free one. The linesman made the decision and the replay later showed that it had probably gone over the line, but how he could be sure isn't clear. After that, I thought Karel had won us a penalty. He is slight and he goes down easily sometimes, but the replay showed that Srnicek did hit him.

Even so, at the beginning of the second half, it did look with Karel's header that we could still get something from this game. I came on for Ronny Johnsen and suffered through the last twenty-five minutes. It turned into one of those days when everything went well for our opponents and nothing really went right for us. I suppose the last goal really summed it up. Albert chipping Peter: you probably won't see something like that again, I thought to myself. When this kind of thing happens, you just have to take your medicine and get on with it. It is only three points, after all, though it puts a big dent in our goal difference. Newcastle made a special video to celebrate, as if they'd won the League already. People were keen to write us off last season when we lost 3–1 to Villa and 4–1 to Tottenham, but we don't think of things that way. We would never write ourselves off after one match.

Immediately after the game, I was really very angry and the coach journey back was miserable. I decided that I wasn't going to go out all week, just go straight home and stay there. But, well, you have to go out and face the world. I seemed to get through the week after the game without too many encounters with Manchester City fans, but you have no idea how many Newcastle fans there are in Mobberley, Cheshire.

Later I learned that it wasn't just a bad day for the team. David May's friend travelled to the game and went to pick up the tickets that David had left for him. The process wasn't very speedy (some friends of mine had a similar problem), and while he was waiting, a policeman asked him to move on several times as he was loitering. At this point, David's friend snapped "I'm just waiting for my f***ing tickets!". The officer warned him that there was no need to swear, which he promptly did again. The policeman arrested him and put him in the holding cells underneath the ground and kept him for four hours, with the result that he missed the match and couldn't get home. He offered a taxi driver £70 to take him back to Manchester and was so annoyed when he reached home that he went to the pub to drown his sorrows. Having gone some way to achieving his aim by closing time, he walked out of the door and was run over.

I was very pleased to captain the team for the Coca-Cola third-round match against Swindon on 24 October, and share something with all the great names who have had that honour in the past. The team had undergone major changes. It was a mixture of young players like Michael Appleton, who was making his first-team debut, and regulars like Roy Keane, who was coming back after being out for a few weeks. Phil Neville also returned from injury.

The Swindon players and fans did their best to make it a special occasion. I received a call to ask if I could sort out some tickets for the Swindon players' wives and relatives, who were bringing a coach down. We played quite well, but when we lost a bad goal from a corner where our defending was very poor, I thought we'd be going down to Swindon in two weeks' time. That was before Paul Scholes put in the winner. Paul has been the most unfortunate of the emerging young players. He went from scoring goals regularly last year for the first team to not even making an appearance, so I was very pleased for him that he won the Man of the Match award. Karel had a purple patch for 15 minutes. There were many positive things and, if there had not been a series of spectacular misses in the final minutes (one of which came from my boot), the scoreline could have been five or six.

The next tie in the competition was against Leicester, but the manager's thoughts about the team for that fixture were impossible to predict. The crowd was excellent – 49,000 – which shows that when tickets go on open sale, people who can't gain entrance for the regular Premiership matches come along and bring their children. The comparison with the Port Vale match two seasons ago is ironic. Then, there were many complaints about the "sub-standard" team Alex Ferguson fielded. As many of those players are now England internationals or first-team regulars, I don't imagine that complaint will be repeated. The crowd here seemed to enjoy watching players who will be stars of the future.

Between the Swindon Coca-Cola Cup tie, and our League match at The Dell, I was to be the guest at the Independent Manchester United Supporters' Association meeting and planned to take Peter Schmeichel along with me. If any difficult questions came up, I intended to merely turn to him, say, "Peter... ?" and wait for him to hiss under his breath (in that gentle way he has), "I will get you later for this." I was looking forward to the meeting: there is always a place for the whole gamut of people who follow United to have a voice. The meeting did not go unnoticed. I arrived early for our pre-match meal before Swindon and walked into the room where we normally eat to find myself in the tail end of a board meeting. Of course, I immediately went to leave, apologising profusely, but the Chairman said, "Come in, you may as well stay as you seem to be involved in everything else at this club anyway." They asked me about the IMUSA meeting. "So you're addressing them?" they said, as if I was leading the meeting, rather than just answering questions as a guest. My reputation as Red Choccy precedes me.

As it turned out, Peter and I enjoyed the IMUSA meeting enormously. We were given a warm welcome and answered questions for about an hour and a half. There were no banal ones, but neither were there any which were particularly controversial. We had agreed beforehand that there would be no written reports of the meeting, so that maybe we could answer questions more frankly than we might otherwise. We promised to take some of the points mentioned back to the other players, including complaints that some of the team didn't wave to our fans in acknowledgement at the end of Newcastle match. One question Peter wouldn't answer was what passed between

Alan Shearer and himself after said game. The audience covered quite an age range, with younger fans and older supporters united by their concern for the club.

The match at The Dell on 26 October was similar to the Newcastle match, everything that could go wrong for us, did. We lost the first goal when Nicky Butt was injured (in an incident which was possibly a penalty but wasn't given), and we lost some of our shape in defence. Nicky couldn't continue and I came on. Within five minutes, Roy tackled the opposing centre half and the referee decided it warranted a booking. I hadn't even noticed that he had been booked for dissent earlier. His sending off seemed very harsh; he had put in a tackle, not a foul, for the second yellow card. Things were very difficult from then on. We pulled one back, but conceded a terrible goal just before half time.

We started the second half very brightly and were rewarded with a goal to make it 3–2. For a time it seemed that we could easily get a draw, but then tiredness set in and some cruel things happened. Once their fourth goal went in we lost our discipline completely. The game was described as a bit of a drubbing, but our performance wasn't as bad as the scoreline suggested. At least we could comfort ourselves with the thought that we brought pleasure to thousands all over the country.

Both the Newcastle and the Southampton results made the front pages of even the broadsheets and were the subject of comment on programmes as wide apart as Film Night and TFI Friday. Our Gaffer appeared rather exasperated by the national rejoicing, but it amused me. I was involved in an unlikely bit of needle with, of all people, Matthew Le Tissier, who aimed a punch at me which neither I nor the referee saw. A friend of mine watching the game confirmed afterwards that this did happen. I went for the ball and, unintentionally, I probably fouled him, but I didn't try and kick him as I've given that up. There followed a minor tussle and he became rather annoyed. It was at that point, I'm told, that he took at swipe at me and missed. I just said to him, on the subject of the challenge, "Look, do you seriously believe that I am going to do you?" He must have seen the logic of this, as a few minutes later we kissed and made up. Thankfully his punches aren't as accurate as his chips. I resolved to say nothing more on the subject of chipping since my prediction for the Newcastle match went so awry.

It's either fate or perversion: when this current United team is really successful and we have a choice about which route to take, instead of zooming straight along the motorway we end up travelling by the B roads and up mountains. We believe in doing it the hard way. We'd done the easy part by winning in Turkey, so back at Old Trafford just a draw against Fenerbahçe would have been good enough. We lost.

Neither side looked as though they could score and, just as things looked as though they weren't going too badly, Fenerbahçe's winner came courtesy of a wild ricochet off David May, which spun into the air and could have gone anywhere. Though the goal was officially credited to Bolic, it needed a lot of help to hit the net. So we arrived at the point where we had to beat Juventus or, failing that, face a tricky tie away to Vienna. We still believed that we had a good chance of getting through to the quarter finals. Our proud, 40-year record of never losing a European match at Old Trafford was lost that evening, and it was not an easy thing to accept. It was going to be broken sooner or later, though. We'd had several narrow escapes in previous years: Lee Sharpe's late equalizer against Barcelona springs to mind. That the record should go because of a freak deflected goal was difficult to take. The romance and kudos of losing to Juventus after a classic match would have been much more acceptable. But I suppose it's far more likely that you will lose it in a much more prosaic fashion, when someone sticks their leg out and the ball flies off into the net. David May could find himself the answer to an interesting quiz question in years to come. "Who was it who scored the goal which ended United's 40-year unbeaten run in European home games?"

Newcastle, Swindon, Southampton, Fenerbahçe. Was this a major slump? A turning point in United's fortunes? No one could say, but if you looked beyond the scorelines maybe it wasn't so clear-cut. Against Newcastle and Southampton, everything went into our net, but curiously we felt that we played quite well. Against Fenerbahçe, it was not a good performance, and though we never looked like losing the game we were overcautious and tentative.

The slide seemed to be accelerating when, the following Saturday, we allowed Chelsea to improve their fantastic record at Old Trafford. For the six years of our recent success, we've become known for not losing goals from set pieces, and in this game we gave Michael Duberry a free header for the first goal. Peter was very disappointed with himself for letting that one in. For their second goal, we were caught trying to play offside. The ball played through to Vialli was superb but there is a school of opinion that Peter should have come out and smothered it, and I'm inclined to agree. But he makes his decisions as he sees them and I've never had a bad game from the sidelines. Perhaps if he hadn't been chipped in the last two matches he would have done. As every footballer knows, if you want to wind up a goalkeeper you chip them. We all try to do it in training and they hate it. It offends their dignity. Still, it doesn't do much for your dignity when someone puts the ball through your legs either, as Vialli did.

Speaking of dignity, I had considerable problems holding on to mine after my team mates read David Meek's interview with me in the programme. Firstly he described me as completely laid back, a mistake if ever there was one. But also, to my colleagues' delight, I was quoted as saying that I try as hard in training as I have always done. I see nothing wrong in this statement, but I was the only one who appeared to agree and suffered for it mercilessly.

Newcastle have pulled their Reserves out of the Pontin's League this season to save their pitch, so we didn't have a Reserve fixture on the Wednesday. Instead, we flew to Norwich for Bryan Gunn's testimonial game. Our transport was booked with a small charter company operating out of Manchester airport. The last time we used their services, the company had its own separate building, but this has been knocked down for the extension of Ringway's domestic terminals. As far as I could tell, I was the only United person in the terminal and, in the growing belief that I had got something very wrong, I asked where the check-in desk was. It turned out to be a phone on the wall. One plane belongs to Jackie Stewart, the ex-racing driver, who lets the company use it. Probably on the principle that you shouldn't put all your eggs in one basket, we travelled in two small aircraft with the manager and the senior players in the smallest. The conditions were very turbulent and the flight a bit of a nightmare.

The game itself was sold out and we played at a good tempo. Our team included Steve Bruce and Eric Cantona. But we had a difficult job to match the excitement generated by the entertainment which preceded us, a dog display. I believe that they were rather good, running around and jumping through hoops. They say that you should never work with animals, and we soon became very aware of another reason why you wouldn't want to follow performing dogs on to a football pitch. The ball boys and girls found that they had an additional duty which may have dimmed the glamour of serving the club on this special occasion.

Given the choice, I might have cleared the pitch myself rather than getting back on the plane for the return journey. Jim Ryan had a particularly bad moment when he couldn't see the runway as we came in to land. Several hours later, they managed to loosen his grip on the seat so he could go home.

5

Old scores

"What's the difference between
a Scotsman and a coconut?"

Wednesday 6 November marked the tenth year of Alex Ferguson's managership at Old Trafford and the *Daily Mail*, one of the two newspapers along with the Express which our Gaffer still allows us to have at the Cliff, asked me to give an interview. Somewhere along the line, most of the tabloids have committed some offence in their coverage of the team which, in the Gaffer's opinion, merits a ban. I was in demand because, as one paper put it, "Who would know him better?" Well, I can think of several people. I asked for the fee to be donated to two Manchester hospitals so something good has come out of his ten years here.

Alex Ferguson has two great qualities as a manager, in my eyes. The first is that when it comes to making decisions he just makes them, whether it's picking the team or buying a player. He makes up his mind and that's it. He doesn't agonize or prevaricate. If the decision he makes is wrong, he holds up his hands and says he's made a mistake. Tactically there have been times when you could fault him, but his successes have proved him right in the long term. His team selection is never made on an emotional basis but on cold, hard logic and he leaves any other problems which might arise because of this until later. If you don't like what he does, you can go and see him afterwards and he'll try to explain his thoughts. But you won't change his mind.

Old scores

He plays the role of a god in the careers of United players. Every one of his decisions can have enormous consequences for each of us. He is extremely tough mentally and able to stand up to the repercussions of what he does, and he expects players to do the same. I get along with him – if I didn't, he would have got rid of me long ago because of some of the things I have said to his face – but the rumours about me being his son are unfounded. I've appreciated that I can always go and speak to him if I've felt it necessary, though I may not always have liked what he's said, and I know this has been true for other players. He's said that once players leave the club they are dead to him as they can no longer be of use to Manchester United, but that's not true. If you have given him loyalty and respect and leave for a good reason, he will help you if he can. He has become so influential and is so respected in the game that he can do a great deal for you. But if you cross him or are disloyal, you forfeit that honour.

He refuses to wash United's dirty linen in public. Privately, if he believes they deserve it, he will discipline players so they don't forget. He is bad-tempered but he doesn't throw things or hit anyone – in fact he hasn't got close to it, and no one has ever hit him. It is a very emotional game and he is an emotional man. But people make the mistake of not realizing that often what he says in interviews may be deliberately for effect rather than in the heat of the moment. A story that best sums up his competitive side is one from when we went to Japan about six years ago. We were training in the driving rain under a motorway where there was some shelter. We were having a game of head tennis, the Gaffer's team versus Archie Knox's (his then assistant). Archie's team won and he told them to go back to the coach, only for them to be called back by the Gaffer who had blown his top. We had to play until his team won, and we probably would be playing still if they hadn't.

His second greatest quality is simply that he is lucky.

I've been at Old Trafford almost as long as the Gaffer. For me, joining United was a long, drawn out affair. Many clubs came in with offers for me in 1987 and Davie Hay, the Celtic manager, had told me I could leave if I wanted. I wasn't really sure about what step to take next. My mind was made up for me when Davie was sacked and Billy McNeill returned for his second spell as manager at Celtic. There were some misunderstandings between us. Alex Ferguson made great efforts to induce me to come to England and to United in particular. When I was an apprentice at Villa, I had only been to Manchester United once. I was taken there to lay out the kit, and watched both teams draw 3–3 in a fantastic game played in lashing rain – so I always believed what they said about the weather in Manchester.

Cologne was one of the clubs which approached me in 1987, but at the time my daughter Siobhan was so young we didn't want to move abroad. It was difficult enough moving to a foreign country like England. I spoke to Chelsea and Tottenham, but in the end I went where the football was best, not where the highest sums of money were offered to me. I have a romantic streak. The Gaffer's interest was also highly flattering. My fee was a knock-down price, fixed by tribunal. Billy McNeill was furious that a striker who had just won a golden boot was judged to be worth £850,000, rather than the £2 million he had wanted.

My goal scoring in the first season at United (twenty-four League goals, thirty-one altogether) and the team's second place in the old First Division was a dream start, and much better than I could have expected. I put my first goal for the club away very early on, against Watford at Old Trafford, and followed it up by scoring ten goals in eleven games. Off the field, my family settled down here very easily; Gordon Strachan and his wife were especially kind and helpful to us.

The fairy story was not to continue strictly according to the script. The excellent football of 1987/88 wasn't repeated in the next few seasons. We believed at the time that we had a team which might have been capable of winning honours and breaking Liverpool's monopoly. However, the manager had a plan in his head and was resolved on radical, long-term reorganization, even if it meant getting rid of some players who were fans' favourites and many others besides. He reduced the playing strength from fifty to thirty five. I think it took Alex Ferguson some while to get a picture of how big a job he had here, and what it meant. Maybe he broke up that first team too quickly. But then he bought Gary Pallister, Neil Webb and Paul Ince when he realized that, compared with Aberdeen, he had the cash available and should spend it – even if it took him beyond £850,000!

They were very turbulent times. In 1988/89, United achieved a final place of eleventh, but topped that in 1989/90 by finishing thirteenth (though we did win the FA Cup after a replay against Crystal Palace). The worst point of my United career in terms of play came when we went eleven League games without winning during the 1989/90 season. We knew we were a good team, but when you get into that kind of run it's not about ability. It becomes a dogfight. We had to go to The Den and take on Millwall for our next game, with a team of young players. We won that day because of our determination, rather than skill.

I hadn't scored a goal for four months until the next game, an FA Cup tie against Newcastle United. It wasn't all plain sailing from then on, but we managed to win enough games to give us a buffer and avoid being sucked into the relegation zone. We did have some success, but the early season experience was frightening. It's incredible now to look back and see that we lost seventeen games in that season in the League. Six is our limit now. I wonder if the young players here can really appreciate how good it is to win a Championship when they've not reached a nadir like we did in 1989/90? You can't get too carried away ever when you know that, if you don't start winning, one moment you're second, the next halfway down the table, and then you're looking at relegation. There was an improvement in the 1990/91 season; we finished sixth and won the European Cup Winners' Cup in Rotterdam. Disappointment at our second place in 1991/92, which I helped to achieve with some of the twenty-six goals I scored, was eased by our League title in 1992/93 when I was, as they say, "ever present". My role then had to change; my days as an automatic first-team choice were over.

If this was the perfect story, I would still be occupying the number nine shirt and scoring twenty-plus goals a season. But that wouldn't just be perfect, it would be miraculous. I'm happy with the number thirteen I have now. After all, I chose it myself.

While the first team did their best to flatten the champagne for the Gaffer's celebrations, the Reserves conjured up a far more fitting tribute in their game against Nottingham Forest at the City ground. The match was brought forward to 9 November, as once again the international weekend allowed us to play on a Saturday. Forest had an unusual way of warming up which intrigued me greatly. Our players were kicking the ball around as per usual, but the Forest men began with a routine of different types of running and then stopped and marked off a little area twenty by twenty. They finally got some footballs out and each one had to knock the ball forward and make a run. This was followed by what looked like five-a-side netball without the nets, in which each player had to take one step and throw the ball. Meanwhile, we continued kicking the ball about. We won the game 4–0. Ryan Giggs was making his return after injury and looked back to his best. There was a hat-trick from Erik Nevland, who was on trial from Norway, and had made quite an impression in the two games he played for us; he had already scored a hat-trick for the A team. Michael Appleton scored a bizarre goal. He was right through, running on to a pass from a ball which I had threaded through, with only the goalie to beat. He looked one way and was going to hit the ball the other, but he slipped and knocked the ball with his right foot. It hit his left and spun up over the keeper's head into the net, and we both fell about laughing.

The following Friday, I was at Old Trafford after training, sorting out various things, and was surprised to find the lounges and conference suites packed with people. There was an electrical cabling exhibition and conference with hundreds there. This is another side of Old Trafford, to which we players are usually oblivious. Occasionally we notice small, cryptic, paper signs to direct delegates to various meetings. Inadvertently, I ended up walking through and disturbing the lunches of 300 or so men, when all I was trying to do was to get round the ground without running into the club tour as I would have to sign autographs and was in a hurry. I stopped at one point to ask the staff, who were ready to serve mounds of fried potatoes and chicken, what was going on. I was startled to learn that for them it was their busiest day of the year and that it had no connection with football, except its location. Apparently the ground is now one of, if not the, most popular conference centres in the North West. Eric would have caused mayhem, but one unshaven Scotsman only made the diners pause a little as a flicker of recognition passed over their faces. "Wasn't that...?"

I held the door open for a young lad carrying the biggest tray of cut-up pork pies I have ever seen, making its way to the other rooms where the lower orders in the cabling world were gathered. He offered me a piece, but the words of a particular terrace song ran through my mind, and I declined.

One day we will play against Arsenal and absolutely nothing controversial will happen. Our latest encounter with the North London club was at home on 16 November. As always seems to be the case in recent years, the match was overshadowed by the row which followed it. Now it seems you don't just have to wait for the referee's report on a match, you also have to hang on for the lip reader's. The allegations about Peter Schmeichel making racist comments to Ian Wright filled the papers for days afterwards. Peter did swear at him – you don't need to be able to lip read to work that out – but he is adamant that he said nothing racist.

At half-time, I went over to stand in the tunnel to watch as the teams came off and make sure that there was no trouble. The tunnel hasn't been the calmest of places on previous meetings between our two sides. Nigel Winterburn, my old sparring partner, walked by and said, "It makes a change from me and you, doesn't it?"

As for the football, it was quite an even game and both sides could have won. In the end we were grateful for Nigel's unfortunate own, but match-winning goal. As a fellow professional I felt for him, just as, in 1988, he commiserated with me on my unfortunate penalty miss against Arsenal in the FA Cup. If I had scored that last minute penalty, rather then blasting it over the bar into the North Bank, we would have equalized. Instead, we were eliminated from the competition in a season when we felt our best chance lay in the Cup.

Some might say that there is bad blood between the two teams.

If you adhere to conspiracy theories, you could say it all began in 1986, the season before I came to United. Apparently, Norman Whiteside mixed it with two of the Arsenal players at Old Trafford in the first five minutes and they completely lost control of themselves. Archie Knox was threatened. In 1988, as I said, Nigel's kind thoughts as I blazed what would have been a match-saving penalty over the bar kept the wound open. In 1989, I had what could be called a falling-out with Winterburn. The ball came out of the box and was dropping to me. Out of the corner of my eye I saw him coming towards me like a train. There was no way he was going to get the ball, so I had to avoid him. I jumped to stop being hurt and he ran straight into me. He was lying down and I got it into my head that he was pretending to be knocked out, so I grabbed him by the shirt and shook him just like a doll, shouting my head off. Then I let him go and he dropped flat and I just walked away. When Brian Kidd is feeling particularly low he can always raise his spirits by reminding me of this incident. The events of 1990 we have already covered. I would stress, however, that there is no real connection between these incidents. They should be seen in isolation, rather than as symptoms of a festering sore.

The best moment of the match came when there was an announcement for the crowd to sit down, and 50,000 people promptly stood up. It brought to a head much of the frustration expressed by fans for two or three seasons now. There are so many restrictions on their behaviour that many supporters are concerned that it is virtually impossible to generate any atmosphere or for fans to get behind the team. Alex Ferguson has been prominent in urging our supporters to rekindle their ardour, but can that ever happen when everyone has to stay in their seats? Many people who come to Old Trafford have learnt their spectatorship in front of the television. They watch a live match in a very similar way, expecting to see all the action and cheering when goals are scored, but they tend to sit in silence when things go wrong. It isn't just at Old Trafford that we have witnessed this effect. Increasingly, the noise comes from the away fans, who are concentrated in one section and are allowed to behave with more freedom than home supporters. Maybe crowds have off days like teams and can't always perform to order.

For the Arsenal match, the club found an answer to the flat atmosphere. Rather than having flag days, tell people not to do something – namely, not to sing. It was really excellent to see such mass disobedience; the buzz around the stadium was tremendous. "Stand up for the Champions," they sang, and stand up they did – for the whole of the rest of the match. Of course, that didn't please those whose view of the pitch was blocked. The choice now is between either accepting a more restrained (but disappointing and passive) atmosphere as the norm, or the creation of special singing and standing sections. Many different types of supporters come to the football nowadays and they have different expectations from fans of a decade or two ago. Everyone has to be catered for. When I'm not playing I don't sit down on the bench but stand at a point near the halfway line (except for European ties where this is not allowed and I have to stand up in the dugout). I consider it my one-man protest.

However, I am also not one of those people who hanker nostalgically after "the old days", whatever those were. There are aspects of the modern game which are frequently denounced, but are essential for its survival and well-being. The sponsorship given to the club by Sharp is one example of how such a partnership can be enormously beneficial.

How important is crowd response to the way players perform? I once played in a game, between Celtic and Atletico Madrid, which had no spectators. Two Celtic fans had been accused of attacking Rapid Vienna's goalie during their European Cup tie replay against Celtic at Old Trafford, and as a result, UEFA decreed Celtic's next European match the following season should be played behind closed doors. It was four o'clock in the afternoon and the only spectators on the empty terraces were the stewards. It was the only time I have ever experienced playing in a virtually empty ground, and it's not one I would like to repeat. It was awful. In the eerie silence the match was flat and the players became more and more tense. We lost 2–1, to go out 3–2 on aggregate, having drawn the first leg 1–1 in Madrid. The European nights at Celtic were something else. The gates were supposedly 42,000 or so, but it always looked as if there were 60,000 there. People were packed in so tightly they could hardly move. Having a crowd making some noise definitely makes a difference.

Though the 1–0 victory against Arsenal kept us in touch with the leaders in the Premier League, the focus shifted immediately to the Champions' League match against Juventus at Old Trafford the following Wednesday. I had a really good feeling about this match, particularly given the excellent atmosphere which was generated spontaneously, without the aid of a Tannoy announcement. It's a good thing I don't earn my living as a prophet. Juventus started the match even quicker than they normally do, and considerably quicker than they did in Turin. They will swamp you if they are given the opportunity, and that is exactly what we gave them for the first forty-five minutes.

There was a problem for us from the beginning with Phil Neville. Looking back on it, he had cycle shorts on, so his hamstring must have felt a bit tight before the match began, but he wanted to play and you can't criticise him for that. He is only nineteen. Unfortunately he got a hamstring pull and, given the choice of players on the bench, the only thing to do was pull Roy Keane back and bring on the old man. We lost a penalty, of the sort you can't argue with. Nicky Butt made the decision to tackle and there was no doubt that he brought his man down. However, in the second half we couldn't have put in more effort or created more chances, but we had no luck. We felt better afterwards – even though we were absolutely gutted, at least we could be proud of the openings we had made. We knew we had not been disgraced.

Our next match was on Saturday 23 November, probably the coldest day of the year, in the new Riverside stadium against Middlesbrough. The biting wind lowered the already freezing temperature. The massive oil-processing factory ship behind the ground was picturesque, but failed to distract us from the brain-numbing temperatures. Our Norwegians were delighted at this reminder of their homeland, and could hardly be stopped from breaking into some of their wonderful whaling songs. Middlesbrough had been struggling for points, and we kindly donated one with a 2–2 draw. As we had a problem with full backs, John O'Kane and Michael Clegg came in from the Reserves. Maybe that little lack of experience caused the second goal, which came from a penalty, but I don't think that I'm being biased when I say that the indirect free kick and resulting penalty was a strange decision. Paul Scholes came out to charge down the free kick and the ball bounced up off his knee and hit his arm. We really should have won this game. I came on for the last two minutes – just time enough for my body temperature to plummet to a level which was extremely uncomfortable, if not life-threatening. I didn't even touch the ball.

Cynics will say that we made our now customary early departure from the Coca-Cola Cup, after losing to Leicester by two goals on Wednesday 27 November. We fielded a team composed of squad players with a few first-team regulars, and we played some reasonable football. We did our best to win, despite what many people will think. For the young players who were in the team this was a big game and they put in an enormous amount of effort. Scholesy missed a penalty; if he had scored, we would probably have gone on to victory. I lost my chance to win the mountain bike for Man of the Match for another year. The last time I won that honour in this competition, the prize was a watch and a bomber jacket with Coca-Cola on the back. Ever since 1992, the Coca-Cola Cup, or League Cup as it was then, has had a bitter-sweet taste for United fans. We won the Cup in that year and I scored the only goal in the final against Nottingham Forest – with the hundredth goal of my United career. However, our involvement in that competition led to six games in eleven days. The fixture pile-up was cited as a major reason for our second place in the Championship. Our Cup victory was not seen as a consolation then, and it still isn't now.

I don't know if it's just a peculiar knack of mine, but I've played some of my best football in years when my club has not realized its full potential. My 41 goals for Celtic in 1986/87 counted for nothing, and only one of my 26 goals in the 1991/92 season for United secured a trophy.

The morning after the Coca-Cola Cup game, I went to pick up Ben Thornley. He said to me, agog, "How's Pally?"

"You know," I said, "Same as always... tight, rude."

"No, no," he went on, "What about his car accident? I heard about it on the radio."

When we got into training, Pally was there and he looked all right. Allegedly, the other driver involved in the accident had jumped a red light and Gary had driven into him. For someone who, according to the wild rumours sweeping Manchester, had been in a coma, he looked fine.

Andy Cole had frustrating news from the specialist. He's been coming along nicely but it is very difficult to say how long it will take before he returns to football. Being impatient to return after an injury can ruin your recovery. Once you start playing again, you forget any idea about being careful, steam in and risk doing yourself a great deal of damage.

On Monday, we had the Annual General Meeting of the PFA. The management committee meets regularly, and the day before the AGM we discuss all the matters that might come up. There are legal cases going on all the time, so we have updates on these. An accountant came in and went over the figures in the afternoon. We'll have to change the timetable; if we'd seen him in the morning session, we might be able to give it a bit more attention. As it was, it just went over everyone's

August 1996, Old Trafford: Manchester United 0, Internazionale 1. "We were reminded of t it takes to be successful in Europe, and it was a good lesson for the younger players."

Pre-season friendly, 28 July, Tolka Park: League of Ireland XI 1, Manchester United 4.
"In Ireland we have an enormous and dedicated following, and the players love to visit."

"David May has professed himself a great
admirer of my wit, without really having
any choice in the matter."

17 August 1996, Selhurst Park: Wimbledon
0, Manchester United 3. "Beckham miss-hit
a cross from 50 yards and scored a third."

21 August 1996, Old Trafford: Manchester United 2, Everton 2. "I didn't know about the Gaffer's little two-step with Brian Kidd out on the pitch until I read the morning papers."

Sharing a joke with Andy in Turin.

Talking tactics with Eric in Istanbul.

11 September 1996, Stadio Delle Alpi: Juventus 1, Manchester United 0. "Afterwards we were really quiet... In the dressing room there had been nothing to say."

"In the second half of the game in Turin, I don't think I gave a bad account of myself."

20 October 1996, St James' Park: Newcastle United 5, Manchester United 0.
"You have no idea how many Newcastle fans there are in Cheshire."

26 October 1996, The Dell: Southampton 6, Manchester United 3. "At least we could comfort ourselves with the thought that we had brought pleasure to thousands all over the country."

"Another glittering night. Myself, David May, Raimond van der Gouw, Brian Kidd, Andy Cole and Phil Neville opened a new Hugo Boss store in Manchester. In the absence of the real stars, I got to hold the tape. Andy cut it and we all smiled and smiled."

23 October 1996, Old Trafford: Manchester United 2, Swindon Town 1.

27 November 1996, Filbert Street: Leicester City 2, Manchester United 0.

"The standard fantasy indulged in by most footballers is that if they weren't players they would be rock stars. Lee Sharpe had a drum kit which he leathered unrhythmically in half-hearted persuance of this dream."

8 December 1996, Upton Park: West Ham United 2, Manchester United 2. "If you do that again, I'm not giving you your signed Man United strip."

"Where are your forks?"

20 November 1996, Old Trafford: Manchester United 0, Juventus 1. "In the second half, we couldn't have put in more effort or created more chances, but we had no luck..."

head after the first ten minutes. We also discussed the current issues in football, like the Bosman ruling, and where we stand. There are other meetings as well, for example the Education Society, which funds various courses.

I became involved with the Scottish PFA when I was a very young player at Motherwell. Under the guidance of Tony Higgins, I was chair for some years. I have always considered it important to be involved in the wider decision-making process in football. I was asked to put myself forward for the PFA Management Committee by my friend Pat Nevin, the current chairman of the English Association, presumably because he thought I might be of some use.

I've been the PFA rep at United since Colin Gibson left for Leicester City in December 1990, and basically I'm there so that people can come to me if there is a problem. If I can't help out myself, I can phone the office and speak to Brendan Batson, Mick Maguire or Gordon Taylor if he's there. We haven't had many problems at Old Trafford because the manager terrifies everyone. There's no point in arguing with him: he's always right. The other duties of the PFA rep are to squeeze the subs out of everyone and to get them all to fill in the Player of the Year forms. My favoured approach is to let nobody leave until it is done, but this present lot take it very seriously and are possibly over-punctilious in their desire to be unbiased. It wasn't always thus. Gordon Strachan chose all Scottish players. Others would fill in the ugly team (in their opinion), or some variant on those lines.

We had another tie against Leicester three days after the Coca-Cola Cup match, but this time it was at home and we were up to strength. What a boring game! They came for a draw and they nearly got it. The manager told the team to go wide down the wings, as this was the only way to get through the packed defence. Eventually, this was where the first goal came from, as Roy Keane broke down the flank and crossed to Nicky Butt. It looked as if it was an own goal from the goalkeeper, but

I was quite delirious on the bench when it went in. They created a few half-decent chances before we scored. But it was really dull and not very pretty. You have to win your home games and we did that, but if you don't score early in matches like this, it will become a stalemate. For the last fifteen minutes we had a proper game of football and four goals were scored. Once again, we had to put thoughts of the Premiership title to the back of our minds: the game to decide whether we were to progress at last beyond the league stage in Europe awaited us.

I'd heard that the pitch in Austria was frozen and had no undersoil heating, so on the Sunday morning, when we were in for training, I asked the kit man if he had dimpled boots. The answer was in the negative. I got him to scoot around looking for them, and he had to tell the guys who get their boots from their sponsors they'd have to pick up some. In the end, we didn't need them even though the pitch was hard. We flew out on Monday and the flight, for once, was uneventful.

The Austrians and Germans have to be the most persistent, thorough fans when it comes to collecting autographs. They keep them catalogued in albums. The fans waiting at the hotel even had a range of pictures of me for signature, one with an alarming amount of grey hair. A particularly eager man pursued me at a run down the hotel corridor, though I was struggling down it with my bags in my hands. I tried to indicate that I would come back and scrawl on his photos once I had put down my very heavy bags, but he wasn't going to afford me any chance of escape. I scribbled something on every one of the six photos he had with him, while trying to stop my arms being pulled from the sockets.

The hotel may have had a glass pyramid (I took my razor blades in to sharpen them) and a swimming pool, but the facilities elsewhere were minimal. My pillow was like an After Eight mint; I had to fold it several times and I didn't sleep well. I thought about making my own pillow by cutting off Karel Poborsky's hair and stuffing it into the laundry bag. Karel sleeps a great deal, though he does get up in time for breakfast. It's odd that every player who rooms with me seems to have no trouble falling into a catatonic state for fourteen hours. I can't think why.

Old scores

Before turning in, we watched sport on the television as Karel really likes it, though he is very amenable if I want to turn to a different programme. He has one English phrase which seems to serve all communication needs: "OK, Choccy". But then again, I know no Czech at all, so he beats me there. At breakfast the next morning, Karel ate his cornflakes with a fork because he hates English milk – presumably because it doesn't come straight from the goat. It is something we share; it would make me sick to drink milk, apart from the merest spot in a cup of tea. We then went to train at the stadium. It was very cold.

When we got back to the hotel after training, Bobby Charlton came over and asked us what had happened. There was a guilty silence as we remembered that he was supposed to have been coming training with us. The manager had told him to be ready at 5.00 pm and we left at 4.15. He'd been sitting in reception in his training gear waiting and we missed him. "Albert," said the Gaffer, "why didn't you tell Bobby when we were leaving?" When in trouble, always blame the kit man.

The next day we had a walk into the pyramid which contained an indoor leisure complex. Then we had a team talk. Even after the Juventus game, I felt we could win if we sorted ourselves out. The Juventus v Fenerbahçe game was being played in Turin simultaneously with our game in Vienna. We spoke in the morning about Juventus, and the possibility mooted in the press that they might field a weakened side against Fenerbahçe. The idea made us laugh. Even without their top stars, the depth of their squad made them formidable. Anyway, it is always a mistake to rely on any else's results. We had to secure our own progression by going for a win.

Our game against Vienna must have been gripping to watch, even if you weren't as involved as I was. There were some great chances for both teams before we scored, then Giggsy put the ball in the net. Vienna's weakness was that they didn't have anyone as quick as Giggs. We knew at half-time that Fenerbahçe were losing to Juventus, and we couldn't see the Italians letting their lead slip, particularly as they were playing at home. Then I had to go on. You know that if Roy doesn't get up there's something really wrong; he got carried off and I replaced him. Then Nicky was injured, which meant the game ended on an unfortunate note. Both Keane and Butt getting hurt was a blow, but a small price to pay for finally progressing to the quarter finals of the Champions' League after so many attempts.

Not that victory always looked inevitable in the first half, when I viewed events from the bench. Peter came rushing out of his goal in the sixteenth minute and it could easily have been interpreted as a sending-off offence. Peter didn't touch the ball or the player and the crew from ITV said that the referee made the right decision. But it just looked daft and the result of a real rush of blood to the head of the normally placid Dane. Jordi complained on the bench when one of the Rapid players rolled over theatrically, but I said, "It's no different from Spanish players." He didn't rise to the bait; he agreed that Spanish footballers would dive to win a game, but British players wouldn't as they are too honest.

This is a familiar belief held by British footballers that, whatever the faults of their game, it is largely honest. Perhaps we're just deluding ourselves, but there is independent confirmation. Someone from the old Yugoslavia, who came over pre-season and watched training, told the Reserve team coach that the players didn't know how to fall to get a penalty. It was a fault in our training that needed correcting, he said. The coach didn't know how to answer him.

As for Peter Schmeichel's save to deny Rene Wagner's header, it looked fantastic. But to call it "better than Banks'" in the 1970 World Cup would be unfair on Pelé. If Pelé had been on the pitch in Vienna, he would have scored. In the dressing room after the game, we tended to our wounded. Roy's cut was horrible; through the gaping wound, you could see the tendons and arteries and the shinbone. It took forty minutes and nineteen stitches to sew it up, and the stitching was a brilliant job. I watched with admiration, but my offer to put in a few stitches was turned down.

Despite his goal against Vienna, the topic on every pundit's lips continued to be Eric Cantona's loss of form. A number of ridiculous explanations have been offered – for instance, that his game has suffered since he became captain – as if having a piece of elastic on his arm has made him overbalance. No matter how good a player you are, you go through periods when things don't go too well. You can't switch it on and off. There's no reason why you are not playing well, why you decide to make the wrong pass or you miscontrol the ball. There are very few players who would have complete confidence in themselves. Jim Ryan says he's only ever known two; one was George Best, the other a Polish player he met in the USA. They were both completely sure of their own ability to play, no matter what kind of patch they were going through.

When other players are not playing well, they adopt a cautious approach and don't try the same things they would when they were on form. Eric doesn't do that. He doesn't change his game; he always shows for the ball or tries to make the pass. Some time soon he'll switch it back on again. He played a lovely ball for Ryan's goal and he scored himself, and yet, acc- ording to some, he isn't playing well. In the manager's eyes he's con-tributing and has an influence which justifies his continued selection.

Sunday 8 December was my birthday and this year, as a special present, I was allowed to play against West Ham. We played in a different formation as we had a few injury problems. Myself, David Beckham and Ryan Giggs made up the midfield but I was supposed to have a more defensive role. We played poorly but despite that, we found ourselves 2–0 up. Even though we lacked coherence, we put together a couple of fluent moves and our goals were excellent.

By the time the second one went in, we had begun to feel the most comfortable we had been all match, passing the ball with more like our usual accuracy, so the disaster which happened next was an even greater shock. We gave away a terrible goal and conceded a penalty though we should never, ever have lost that lead. No team should do it. I don't think we've lost a game for a long time when we've been 2–0 up. We didn't lose this time, but it was definitely two points dropped.

West Ham's Iain Dowie, who is on the PFA Management Commit-tee with me, had asked me to get a strip signed for him, which I did. He must have phoned me at least three times in the week before the match to remind me. "Don't panic," I reassured him, "I've done it." I didn't hand it over before the game. In the first half he went down in the box and in my opinion he threw himself down looking for the penalty. So there he was, lying on the pitch with me standing over him berating him sternly for diving. I saw him at half-time and said, "If you do that again, I'm not giving you your strip." Iain was all injured innocence. "Brian, I was pushed!" he protested. One of us was right.

The away dressing room at Upton Park is at the front of the ground, and people can walk along by it. Fans can actually see down into it. During the sacred moments that are the team talk, it was very warm in there and we opened the window to let in a bit of air. West Ham fans were looking in and shouting out while the Gaffer was holding forth. Someone boomed out, "What's the difference between a Scotsman and a coconut? You can get a drink out of a coconut." The manager had been concentrating so hard on what he was saying, he didn't hear what had been said to make his players fall about laughing. Brian Kidd repeated it and the Gaffer joined in the laughter.

His good humour, unsurprisingly, did not survive the last twenty minutes of the match. He was very, very angry with us – with every reason. This time there was plenty of shouting, and we deserved every bit of what came our way. His post-match interview showed how he felt, including the comment that Beckham's goal was a fluke and he wasn't aware that Peter had made two very good saves at the end of the game.

What is the point of doing post-match interviews? If you've won, you're only going to be asked banal questions and your answers will sound smug. If you lost, you don't feel like replying and there's always the possibility that a reasonable question will hit a raw nerve. In either event, you're never asked a question that doesn't contain the answer, thus: "So you've been drubbed 5–0. You must be really disappointed..." And what a sensational coach journey we had back to Manchester.

Our Premier League form continued to lack any fluency, and we maintained our run of disappointing draws against Sheffield Wednesday at Hillsborough ten days later. It absolutely poured down all Saturday. I might even have started a match this time as Scholesy, who should have been playing, had been slightly injured in an A-team match. But at lunch the manager told me over my tea and toast that I wasn't in the team. "Fine," I told him. It wasn't a very good game; to use the cliché, it was a game of two halves. Sheffield Wednesday had such a powerful start that they could have been three goals up in the first forty-five minutes. Although Giggsy was right through after six or seven minutes, Wednesday had more pressure and more chances. In the second half, as we played going down the hill we had the better opportunities but, irritatingly, we gave away the ball and Carbone scored. (This was ironic, as I had had the role of Carbone – only taller – in our preparation training game for the match.) We came back with a fine strike from Scholes (what a wise choice for the manager to include him in the side), and we just about managed to have more of the play. The pitch was very heavy and by the end of the game most of the men were very tired. It was a really open game, but we had only ourselves to blame for not winning; we gave the ball away with annoying regularity and we passed poorly. I almost made an appearance in the ninety-first minute. Kiddo bet me a tenner that I wouldn't, and he was right.

So we marked our manager's ten year anniversary with what Kiddo would describe as a "mixed bag". In Europe we'd had success, but perhaps at the expense of our domestic progress – though naturally that was not our intention. We'd drawn two matches on the run and overall had tied more matches than usual at this stage of the season. There was no team running away with the Premiership and we had had what the manager called too many silly results. It didn't take second sight to assume that if any club managed to put together a run like the one we started from Christmas through to March in the 1995/96 season, they would win the Championship. At Old Trafford we hoped it would be us, but we'd have to begin against Sunderland on 20 December.

6

Christmas happy

"You know you've just knackered up
all our tactics, don't you?"

Christmas doesn't really make much difference at a football club. Not at this one, anyway – except that the Megastore and the other club shops are stripped bare and are packed even on Sundays. We players don't go in much for celebrations, as for us it's always the time when we work our hardest. We had a very modest Christmas meal last week at a local Italian restaurant we hired for the night. Eric had brought over some musician friends from France, who played rather like the Gypsy Kings, and they were excellent. Even though it was just a quiet meal, there was a photographer waiting for us as we went in. If he was hoping for some incriminating photographs, surely it would have made more sense for him to snap us as we came out. However, we were a sober and respectable crew throughout.

You can imagine how many requests the club normally receives to participate in various charity events, good causes and visits. At Christmas, the number of invitations doubles, and it's impossible to fulfil them all. You can go to the General Office at any time and sign umpteen birthday cards and bits of paper, but when you add Christmas cards as well we're snowed under. If people want signatures they should send requests in well in advance, as much of the time players won't even be at the ground. They might come in once or twice a week and on a match day, and then they're always in a hurry to rush off and do any number of important things – like playing with their PlayStations for several hours or buying expensive but tasteless clothes. Today there were roughly thirty things to sign in the office – balls, posters, strips and cards – but the mailboxes were full and there were more of the grey mail sacks waiting. Kath in Reception always tries to inculcate good habits in the youngest players by encouraging them to answer their post straight away. It's far too late for the older ones, though. The club also insists on approving all the events and projects players are involved in.

Last Thursday, some of the players went to Booth Hall Children's Hospital to hand out presents and have some photographs taken. This week there was a request for a visit to an old folks' home about a hundred yards from the Cliff. The manager had so much to do that he asked me if I would co-ordinate the trip, and four of us went. Gary and Phil Neville both came, but Gary arrived first. The man who ran the place kept calling him Phil, so to save his embarrassment I called Phil Gary. The residents seemed quite happy to have some different people to come and see them, whether we were United players or not. We were only there for about twenty minutes. I think it may have been a mistake to go straight after training, as when I tried to leave, having sat down I couldn't get back up again. One of the men there said to me, "You look a lot smaller on the television." A minute later another observed, "You're smaller than you look on the television." I agreed with them both.

Even the children's Christmas party has changed since Manchester United became such a massive institution. In the last few years the number of employees has almost doubled. In my first years here, the captain of the first team, Bryan Robson, organized the Christmas functions. The adults would go to a local hotel for a fancy dress party for players and wives, which always used to be highly enjoyable. Bryan and his wife Denise also put a huge amount of effort into organizing the children's party. Denise used to buy a present each for all the children of all the employees of the club, and that was quite a large number even before the expansion. The party would usually be on the Sunday afternoon before Christmas and there would be a Santa. But last year there was an unfortunate omission when the children of the employees of one section of the club weren't invited. It wasn't the fault of Steve Bruce, who had taken over organizing the party; he just wasn't aware of this other section. So this year we decided it would just be a small affair for the children of the players and the staff who work at the Cliff. It was a lovely party for twenty or so children; there was a little disco, Father Christmas appeared and they all received a present. My three had been asking me for six weeks when the party was, but Liam refused to dance and entertained himself by kicking a balloon around the dance floor.

We also had a carol service at which I did one of the readings. The YTS lads had to sing a carol and my daughters joined in the staff choir but I, mercifully for everyone else, remained silent. In my youth I was an enthusiastic singer of carols, until it was pointed out to me that I was also very loud and completely tuneless. There was an hour-long service which I enjoyed. Liam again behaved very curiously, and seemed rather temperamental. The mystery was cleared up when he came out after the service smiling with relief and announced, "Great, now I can get my Christmas presents!" It transpired that Laura had told him he wouldn't receive any unless he went to the disco and the service, and that any misbehaviour would definitely result in presents being withheld. Of course, the resulting strain only served to make him tense and irritable.

The other staff event had terrible repercussions for me. We had our traditional Christmas lunch at the Cliff, beautifully cooked and set out by the ladies. They did turkey with all the trimmings. Unfortunately, professional footballers can be a wee bit immature sometimes and someone threw a sprout at one of his team mates. You can guess what happened next. I recorded this briefly in "Choccy's Diary" and the ladies were very hurt. Continuous grovelling seemed to be no use at all. I even dubbed 19 December my "Be nice to women" day, only to have one of the secretaries mumble that she'd have to type out and circulate a memo to publicize it to all females at the ground as they would never notice otherwise. I was eventually forgiven after apologizing in the next instalment of the Diary and learnt my lesson, as usual, the hard way.

Over the Christmas period proper, we had a game against Forest on Boxing Day. This meant travelling down on the Wednesday night, which unfortunately was Christmas Day. We had done the same two years before, when we went to Chelsea. The players were allowed to decide when they wanted to train and the majority were happy with Christmas Day evening, which meant anyone with kids could spend some time with them. The few times I have gone in on the Christmas Day morning, we've had to wake the children up so I can be there when they open their presents, which is rather the wrong way round. Christmas dinner is quite normal, apart from the alcohol. Most of the players eat at home, though a few go out to eat. All of us know that we can't overindulge. There have been some wild rumours in the past about excessive holiday celebrations; it's amazing how the football rumour machine operates. Many ridiculous stories have been told about me, most of them unrepeatable. However, yesterday I was told that I'd been seen drinking lager out of cans in Piccadilly Gardens in the centre of Manchester. I knew I should have chosen somewhere a little less public.

We players don't give each other presents or cards any more as we just became fed up with it. Twenty times twenty cards – we were just passing them around to each other. That's four hundred cards to go into the bin. Now we save each other a fiver. At home, for the first time for many, many years in my pampered existence, I've had to write out my own Christmas cards. Usually Maureen does all that but she has been so busy I had to take on the responsibility. It's awful. Last week I e-mailed some person in Orkney to ask them the Gaelic for "Happy Christmas", to make my Christmas cards more pretentious, but I ended up putting it the wrong way round so now they read "Christmas Happy". I usually sign autographs "Sláinte, Brian McClair", sláinte being Gaelic for "Cheers", but I expect most people think it's some scrawled illegibility.

This year I had even less Christmas spirit than usual; it was almost as if I was trying to block it out and get on with the job. Business went on as normal. The usual debate about a mid-season Christmas or winter break is being trotted out again this year. From a personal point of view (and I'm sure most professionals would agree with me), it would be wonderful if we didn't have games over the Christmas period. Everyone would be prepared to train, but we'd like Christmas Day and New Year's Day off. However, it's a bumper time for the clubs themselves. An awful lot of people want to go to a football match on Boxing Day afternoon, and why should they be deprived?

Even though the Christmas celebrations had to be low key, if we were to keep in touch with the teams at the top of the League, the importance of the matches we faced over the holiday could not be over-estimated. Traditionally, over the last few seasons at least, we become better and stronger as the season goes on, and we were in better shape this year than we were over Christmas 1995. Then, we had the French-man William Prunier, a triallist, at centre half and lost 4–1 to Spurs. This time, we had everyone available apart from Roy and Andy, and they were both back in training. Andy Cole is really due for a change of luck. His return will, I believe, definitely make a difference; we won the double last year with a team playing Andy Cole up front after all. There are many different things that Andy brings to the team that his critics ignore. He runs at defenders and works the opposing back four very hard. You get the feeling that the only way he would be able to silence the critics so keen to dwell on his errors would be to score a hat-trick every match.

The Christmas period proper began on 21 December with a 5–0 victory over Sunderland at Old Trafford. It was better than we could have hoped for, because Sunderland came here after a run of good results and our form had been decidedly patchy. They worked very hard. Their management team always do their homework, and coach and organize their players on the basis of how the opposition play and how they might stop them. They believed they had come up with tactics to stop us, but we played a completely different system. It was just one of the manager's ideas to play differently and I think it confused them. We played three at the back, with Denis, Pally and David May. At half-time we were win-ning 2–0, though Sunderland had started quite brightly. We made a slight change to our formation and scored two goals, one a penalty just before half-time, and that was Sunderland effectively finished. Their tactics were based on the score remaining 0–0; once we scored they had to come out and play. Their Reserves coach, Bryan "Pop" Robson, was Reserves coach at Old Trafford for a while and he said, "You know you've just knackered up all our tactics, don't you?" I don't know whether it was a deliberate tactic, a manifestation of the Gaffer's genius, or an accident.

As Pally aggravated his back injury, I came on in the second half and we began to turn on the style. I made a goal for Eric. No skill was required on the Frenchman's part; he couldn't miss. Actually, he deliberately made the task of scoring look as difficult as possible. He had to let the shot drift in off the wind. The result probably flattered us. I should think Sunderland went home wondering how they came to lose 5–0.

There was a Dutch-style band playing to improve the atmosphere. Opinions are divided about whether it worked or not, and I've already given my thoughts on enforced jollification, but the band might have been more effective if it hadn't been positioned right in front of the away fans. It appeared to give them quite a boost.

The team travelled down to the City Ground on Christmas Day. My family had the Christmas celebrations early, though Maureen and I didn't have to wake our children up as I predicted. Instead we lay in bed ignoring for as long as humanly possible the deafening noise they were making. After forty-five minutes of training, the team boarded the coach. Disappointingly, no one had received any unusual or tasteless presents. In the absence of any interesting videos we amused ourselves by playing with a Sega driving game brought by one of our Norwegians. Two could play at one time, with a split screen. Eric was driving a car for a couple of minutes but appeared to be absolutely hopeless at it. He couldn't seem to stop his car bouncing off every wall. Then it transpired that he had been looking at the wrong side of the screen.

Though Nottingham Forest were struggling at the bottom of the League, Frank Clarke's replacement by Stuart Pearce had seen a revival in the club's fortunes and they had just beaten Arsenal. This often wiped out the Newcastle and Southampton goal deficits.

For the rest of December we continued to get the right results, though not necessarily in the most entertaining way. Our dire home tie against Leeds brought the year to a close. Under George Graham, Arsenal always had the tag of being boring; people may have to start calling his new charges the same thing. But not giving a goal away isn't a bad thing – as our Gaffer is forever reminding us. George Graham has stated that his priority is to sort out Leeds' game defensively. In the four games they played before they faced us, I don't think they'd lost a goal – though they weren't winning either. He played Radebe (who performed magnificently in goal in the 1996 fixture against Manchester United) as a man marker against whoever George considered the most influential player in the opposing team – Zola, Vinnie Jones. For some reason, for United they picked Cantona – I've no idea why. So Radebe followed Eric about and it was a wee bit amusing when he got in the bath with him at the end. The game had a terrible start, the type where they say on the radio that it needs a goal. And then we got a penalty. I think it was the first time this season that we have scored in the first ten minutes and you think, "Great, this game will really be on now," but it got worse. There were only two good bits of football in the entire match: when we were awarded a penalty, and when we scored from it. But Peter was happy to keep a clean sheet and we earned three points. It was a perfect footballing Christmas, with ten points out of twelve.

For two of the squad, the holiday period was not so perfect. In the past, Pally has hardly missed any games for United through injury but recently his good luck has run out. He sat out the Leeds game thanks to a flare-up of his sore back, caused, as far as I understand it, by wear. It will get worse and then improve, then something will jar it and his back will become painful again. There is no degeneration, but he will always have a certain amount of pain. There will be times when he is not able to play and there is no operation which might improve his condition. Many footballers play with pain of varying levels, in their knees or ankles as well as backs. The pain is a fact of their lives.

Today we received a visitation from the ghost of Phil Neville, one of the players who has come into the first team at a very young age. It's obvious that he is a great player and will only improve; he has a marvellous future at United. Phil is exactly what he appears: a level-headed, very pleasant person. Earlier on this season he picked up an ankle injury and missed some training, then over Christmas he contracted glandular fever, obviously from too much kissing under the mistletoe. In an alarmingly short time he lost a stone and a half. As he is under orders to go to McDonald's and eat, he's now the envy of the younger contingent. He says he feel fine but it is difficult to predict when he will recover. Anyone who's had glandular fever knows it can affect different people in different ways, for a few weeks or a few years.

A few days after the Leeds game, we had a players' meeting. Among other topics we discussed the forthcoming free weekend in February, when a branch of the supporters' club was to celebrate an important anniversary. The manager was going and there was some competition among the players about who would accompany him. We drew lots for the honour and the lucky winners were our hearty Norwegian duo, Ronny Johnsen and Ole Gunnar Solskjaer and, in his absence, the still recovering Phil Neville. Naturally, the Gaffer suggested we'd have to choose someone else instead. Phil's older brother decided to do his bit to defend his sibling's interests.

"He's coming into training Friday," Gary piped up.

"Aye, Gary, but there's no guarantee he'll be well enough," rejoined the genius of Old Trafford.

"But he's walking now," added Gary, failing magnificently to do anything to advance Phil's case for a trip to the supporters' club, and merely making him sound like Lazarus.

We welcomed the New Year with an even worse game than the one against Leeds. Against Villa at Old Trafford, there was no goal of any sort to enliven the gloom. Ryan should have scored early in the match but made the decision to volley a ball which, in my opinion, able to be wise after the event, he should have headed. Mark Bosnich had an excellent game, and saved particularly well from Andy Cole. He never makes glaring errors against us, only against Newcastle or Liverpool – which shows he rises to the really big occasion.

The first Old Firm tie of 1997 found me in front of the television as a fan, not a player. When Celtic equalized after Rangers had taken the lead, I shocked myself by jumping from my seat, waving my fist and shouting in triumph while Maureen eyed me coolly from the sofa. Rangers disappointed me by taking the lead again, but the truly painful moment came when a perfectly good goal, superbly taken by Jorge Cadete, was disallowed. The debate over whether the refereeing is partial to the Protestant club started all over again. After the two teams last met at Parkhead, I spoke to someone at Celtic who said the situation with officials was a complete joke in Scotland. His view was that in Old Firm games, Celtic always have to have to beat the referee (and the assistant referees) as well as Rangers. I can't tell anything from just watching the games on the television, and I mistrust my own judgment given that I am one of the Catholic minority. Perhaps we'll have to import impartial foreign officials.

7

Tin cup

"Excuse me, but have any of you been asked
by a guy to send him your dirty socks?"

As almost everyone knows, for the last three years Manchester United
has contested the FA Cup final, so our supporters have re-christened
Wembley "Old Trafford South". The Gaffer should have quite an affec-
tion for this competition too, as our success in the Cup in 1990 is
generally credited with ensuring he was still around to celebrate his ten
years here. Received wisdom has it that if it wasn't for our third round
victory against Nottingham Forest by a single goal from Mark Robins,
following eight games without a win, our Gaffer would have been on
his way out. Our Chairman denies this would have happened, but the
1988/89 and 1989/90 seasons would have been unrelentingly gloomy
without the glitter of that trophy.

Even that Cup win had its shambolic side. Though we had drawn the
final 3–3 by the skin of our teeth, and still had a replay to face, we
nonetheless did the bus ride around Manchester afterwards, without a
trophy. It was terrible weather on the Sunday and it felt even colder on
the open top deck. Maybe the public were misinformed about the times
and the route, maybe they were waiting for us to actually win the Cup
Whatever the reason, the streets were empty for most of the journe
Archie Knox and I amused ourselves by waving at people in blocks
flats half a mile away, just to see if they would wave back. Whenever
got a response, we cheered, "Yeah, I got a wave back!" Since then,

there is hot rice pudding, smaller portions of cold rice pudding and yoghurt and pots and pots of tea.

This Saturday, Eric was drinking his soup and asked one of the girls serving for the pepper. She handed him a copy of the *Manchester Evening News*.

Then we move on to the players' lounge, where the daily papers are laid out and there is yet another TV high on the wall. The players watch television while leafing through the papers. In my first days at Old Trafford several players would put a bet on the horses, but gambling is not the vice of any of the quiet lads we have now. Ralph Milne was tipster supreme in his short time at United. Now David May might occasionally risk a few pence, because he has a good friend who is a jockey. Then we drift down to the dressing room. Some players, if they know they are going to be playing, take their suits off right away as and put on their kit; others wander around and like to take their time getting ready. They might have strapping put on an injury or have a bit of a massage. Usually, the manager comes down and takes one or two of the players up with him to the executive lounges. There, we say hello and hand over a couple of prizes and then do the same thing for Sharp, our sponsors. We share those duties around, so that you might have to do it four or five times a season.

If you have been playing and are going to be dropped (or "rested", as we now call it), the manager summons you to his execution room and tells you his ideas and why you are not in the team – or he'll make something up that sounds good. At half one, we have to go and listen to him preach his sermon which lasts anything between twenty and thirty minutes. The chief aim is to remind us of how our opponents play, what particular dangers they pose, and how he wants us to play to counter this. Then he'll run through free kicks, corners, who's in the wall, who will line it up with Peter and so on. He also has the match reports of the opposition's last three games, which he uses to refresh our memories about which of them takes set pieces and who are the danger men. He ends the talk by naming our side and what he expects each of us to do on the day. Before today's match, David Beckham's mobile phone rang and he jumped miles into the air in his embarrassment. The manager didn't bat an eyelid, merely took it off him and dropped it in the bin. When the talk was finished, the Gaffer announced the subs. I was one of them again for this Cup tie.

At two o'clock the manager goes back to his room and for the players it's merely a question of getting ready. I sit around and read or do a crossword until half past, when most of us go out for the pre-match warm-up. We come back in for a quarter to three. Then come last minute preparations: shin pads, tie-ups and liberal applications of Vaseline on the bits of our anatomy we want to remain unchapped. I rub plenty into my thighs and on my chest, to prevent jogger's nipple, which I am in danger of contracting while warming up endlessly on the sidelines. And we shake hands or exchange hugs in final preparation before we leave the dressing room to go out on the pitch.

I enlivened my pre-match warm-up today (only a gentle one as I wasn't playing) with a brief chat with the ground staff, who were solemnly and ponderously tramping down divots.

"Where's your forks?" I asked.

"We don't bring those out until half-time," came the indignant reply. Their expressions seemed to say, "How can he be so ignorant of the mysteries of pitch preparation after all this time? That's players for you…"

Spurs fielded a young team for this third round tie as they were still bedevilled by injuries. Despite that, the first half was closely fought. As it came to an end, Denis Irwin began to feel his hamstring and during the half-time team talk I was sent out early to prepare for what might be a full second-half substitution if Denis was unable to run it off. The crowd had just finished watching George Best make the cashdash draw. He'd been serenaded appreciatively by the Tottenham fans with the charming ditty, "You're p★★★ed, and you know you are." I felt absolutely ridiculous as I ran out alone, even though I do have something in common with George, as the only United player since his departure to score over twenty League goals in a season. I scored twenty six in 1987/88.

Fifty-five thousand people watched me run up and down the touchline with Fred the Red, the United mascot, who often does mock warm-up exercises. I was worried if I got too close to him, it might prompt unfavourable comparisons. I could have done something really spectacular like sprint along the half-way line, but I bottled it. Instead I jogged over to the ground staff, who were stamping the pitch with even more concentration than before.

"You've still not got any forks," I remarked, observantly.

"Of course not!" one snapped, which led me to believe that the fork story was a cover for what was really a groundsmen's fertility dance. Perhaps they were worm charming. A couple of years ago, the head groundsman did put out an appeal on national radio for blue-nosed worms to improve the state of the pitch; this breed of earthworm is particularly good for soil aeration, apparently. The start of the second half interrupted this fascinating reverie.

Denis was obviously struggling, but after five minutes Paul Scholes scored to break the deadlock. After that we were more comfortable, which meant we could make a change which would alter the team's formation. We were supposed to play three at the back, but I really functioned as a wing back on the left, and began to enjoy quite a bit of space. Though Rory Allen had a great chance to equalize, it never looked as if we were going to lose. David Beckham scored another magnificent goal with a screaming long-range shot. Afterwards we sat and watched the fourth round draw on the box, hoping that Manchester City or Brentford came out of the bag. Instead, we were rewarded with a home tie against Wimbledon.

Our next two League matches saw us take six very valuable points away from home, but the Wimbledon Cup tie seemed to arrive very quickly. The Gaffer and Kiddo had selection problems, because we didn't have any fit centre halves, so Chris Casper played and Roy Keane filled in at the back. Considering the team we had out and Wimbledon's aerial threat, we did really well. I got a game, too. When Paul Scholes scored right near the end, we were congratulating ourselves on having one of those games where it's all gone to plan. You know you've defended well, concentrated for the whole ninety minutes and stopped the other side from playing. Just then, Ole gave away a silly foul and a couple of our players complained about it. Well, players do it all the time – I've certainly been guilty. You say something to the referee, but he's not going to change his mind, is he? "OK then Mr McClair, you've got a reasonable point there – expressed rather forcefully if I may say so, but nevertheless very reasonable. I'll just alter my decision, shall I?"

Wimbledon knocked the resulting free kick into a great area that was very difficult to defend, but in any event the marking was non-existent. No one would own up to the responsibility of marking Robbie Earle – not even in the team talk before the League game the next Wednesday evening, when it was mentioned as it was vital to avoid the same mistake again. And Wimbledon had equalized two minutes before the close of play. Perfect, we thought, a mid-week replay at Selhurst Park in ten days' time. We were very disappointed with ourselves, but it was yet another example of Wimbledon's spirit. Not that United is lacking in that department; we always believe we can salvage a game and the number of last-minute goals we have conjured up for a win or a draw is testimony to that. But when we pull off a victory in the dying moments, we're usually described as lucky rather than tenacious. We wanted to continue in the FA Cup, but the feeling was that as far as possible we should try to go through on the first attempt with no replays.

Eric was booked for diving in this game but it was very harsh. His opponent was running with him and pulling his shirt. I was very confused at the time about what he actually was booked for; he's not a diver.

Before the game kicked off, there was another chapter in an ongoing saga about the music played in the stadium prior to matches and at half-time. One person's all-time top ten is another's cacophony; there would probably be no agreement among the fans themselves about what songs they would like to hear. However, the stadium rock anthems favoured by our DJ, Keith Fane, have come under fire from various quarters. In an attempt to end moans about the stultifying effect of a nonstop diet of

Tina Turner and Queen, Keith switched off his record decks for fifteen minutes before the match and announced that it was up to the supporters to create their own atmosphere. As I've already said, instructing people to do something never works. He should have told them that all chanting and singing of songs had been banned as it was making it difficult for elderly, out-of-town, hearing-impaired supporters to catch the lyrics of "Simply the Best" while unscrewing their Thermos flasks and making the people in front of them sit down. Then, we would all have been deafened by the vocal protest. As it was, you could have heard a pin drop. Keith has also received letters taking him to task for playing records by Oasis, as their more high-profile members are Manchester City fans.

By 5 February, we knew that whatever else happened, there would be no domestic double this year. On the day of the Wimbledon replay, the rain bucketed down at Selhurst Park and if it had continued the referee would have had to have called the match off. Miraculously, it stopped before kick-off. Wimbledon played a system with three forwards, so they were obviously going to take the game to us, and they caused us a lot of problems. There were thousands of United supporters in the ground again. When Wimbledon's goal came, everyone was expecting Vinnie Jones to throw the ball long, but he took a short, clever throw-in which led to a great cross. Despite our best efforts, particularly those of Peter Schmeichel who "scored" with a magnificent (but disallowed) shot on the swivel deep into injury time, we couldn't equalize. It was a terrific finish by Peter, worthy of any forward, but we all know from training that he is capable of that kind of shot. He wasn't the only one offside by any means.

Going out of the Cup was a big disappointment: if we had made it to Wembley again, it would have been our fourth final in a row. You'd have thought that, by the law of averages, there was no way we could win another final. But looking at the teams who had gone out of the competition by the fifth round stage, we would have had a great chance of progressing quite far. Once more I hauled myself off the bench for the last seven minutes and functioned as a one-man defence. This gave me the opportunity to witness a fight between Vinnie Jones and Mick Harford on the pitch. I haven't got a clue what it was about, but I do know that I would not fight Mick Harford under any circumstances. I would have been grovelling in my apologies, whether I had done anything to offend him or not. Eric was so frustrated at one point with our failure to find an equalizer that he kicked the advertising hoardings, and for one moment the spectre of history repeating itself did occur to me.

There was yet another free weekend in the fixture programme, so Eric and I travelled to Aberdeen to appear at a dinner. Once again I marvelled at how popular United are wherever you go, in Britain or elsewhere. People come from all over the country and Europe to work in Aberdeen because of the oil rigs, and they were represented at a question and answer session we took part in. Eric was excellent, revealing to all those present the full significance of his seagulls and trawler aphorism, but until he feels able to share it with a wider public, I guess it will remain a secret. The next day we popped into some retail outlets owned by the man who had sponsored our flights down, to talk to his staff. They were very low key affairs, and some customers had been invited along as well. The manager at one particular store, where Eric had been surrounded by adoring hordes, remembered me after a while. "Naturally," he announced, "it's nice to be able to welcome Brian up here, too. Er, where is Brian?" I was, of course, standing right next to him. A friend of mine collapsed with laughter and declared, "Time to put the bandages back on, Choccy!"

After the flight home I went to Lancaster for a supporters' branch dinner dance and buffet. Maureen had an essay to write for the degree course she started this year, so she didn't mind me disappearing on a Saturday night. It was very enjoyable. I am not noted for my grace on the dance floor, but there was a man there who had the priceless ability of dancing to the previous record. My part in the evening was to move around seventy guests to talk and pose for photographs, for three hours or so. The relatively small number at the function allowed me to spend more time than usual with individuals. Football always gives people plenty to discuss and the conversation was lively, especially when they had had a few drinks and put the questions people wouldn't normally ask if they feel they have to be polite. One of the perks of growing older is that you no longer feel uncomfortable talking to people you don't know – in fact, it becomes something of a pleasure. The organizer sent me a charming letter of thanks afterwards and I felt the satisfaction of a job well done.

The Royal Mail had a bumper delivery to Old Trafford on Valentine's Day. I'm a cynic about it; you can send someone flowers every day of the year but if you should forget them on 14 February... Giggs and Beckham received sackfuls of cards, and the people who grow trees and manufacture cards must love it. Actually, at the Cliff recently, some giggling teenage girls bypassed the usual heart-throbs to gush breathlessly, "Can we have your autograph?"

I naturally obliged and they were quick to express their gratitude.

"Oh, thank you," said one, "My mother will be thrilled, you're her favourite player."

"Yes," added her friend, "And you're my gran's too!"

The most unusual request I ever received from a fan, though you couldn't call it a Valentine, came shortly after I arrived at the club. A man wrote asking if I would send him a pair of my dirty match socks, and he was very insistent that they should be dirty: "Please don't wash them," he stated, "As I like to do that myself." I didn't send him any, though, as it could have been a Sunday newspaper despatching letters to various players to see if they would comply. Thinking about it now, socks seem a bit of a tame article of kit for that kind of set-up, but I didn't conduct a survey among the other players to see if they had received a similar request in the past. It's not really the sort of thing you ask about in the dressing room if you have only been at a new club for a few weeks. I couldn't see myself going up to the likes of Bryan Robson, Norman Whiteside, Paul McGrath, Kevin Moran and Remi Moses – all men you didn't mess around with – and saying, "Er, excuse me, but have any of you been asked by a guy to send him your dirty socks?" No, I don't think so, somehow.

I was pleased to hear a good shopping story today. Dedicated readers of "Choccy's Diary" will know that many of my most enjoyable hours are spent in Sainsbury's, with the occasional foray into Marks and Spencer, punctuated by inexpert DIY. This has led commentators in the fanzines to speculate that in some way I am letting the male side down. The bookies or the pub are considered more suitable venues for a footballer's leisure hours. Well, let me recommend shopping to any young professional who feels they are in danger of going off the rails. Cheaper and with less risk of personal injury than a punch-up outside a nightclub, you very rarely end up with a hangover. Getting behind a trolley is great therapy. Not that footballers' shopping exploits are always received with approbation by their managers. The story of Harry Redknapp's condemnation of Florin Radicioiu, for instance, was doing the rounds. Radicioiu was supposed to be playing for West Ham away to Stockport in the Coca-Cola Cup. Instead, he went shopping at Harvey Nichols with some friends over from Romania, and didn't turn up for the departure of the team bus. Redknapp had him in the office the next day, and told him he was fining him two weeks' wages. "No problem, Harry," said Radicioiu. He was expanding his wardrobe when he should have been playing. Even though I came back from the supermarket today with a bag of someone else's shopping, so great was my enthusiasm, it's hard to credit that he would have turned his back on the chance to be out on the pitch.

8

Dizzy heights

"The quiet tie against Arsenal that
I'm convinced is just around the corner was
not to be this time…"

While we were making fitful and limited progress in the Cup, our
League form continued to show the consistency we had found over
Christmas. By a trick of fate, we found ourselves playing both Spurs and
Wimbledon in the Premier League straight after we had met them in
the Cup competition. We played Spurs again in a Sunday game on 12
January at White Hart Lane and I contracted a stiff neck, even though I
never made it out on to the pitch. The jumbo TV screen they've erected
behind one of the goals at Tottenham ought to be banned. The dugout
is so low that you constantly have to look up to see what is going on,
and it's very distracting. Why should you want to watch the whole game
on a screen as it is happening in front of you? They're putting one on
the other side of the ground as well. You needn't actually look at the
action on the pitch at all – you could just stay in your own home. Often
they replay bits of action while the game is still going on, but curiously
only the parts where Tottenham are doing well.

For this match we had three centre backs and Giggsy was playing
left-wing back, a change of position which he did not receive particularly joyfully. But he'll have to accept that circumstances may dictate this
sometimes. As our Gaffer is a genius, we won 2–1. The three points were
sealed by another wonder goal from David Beckham, who was limping

from an ankle injury and was close to being substituted before he scored. Karel robbed Howells in the midfield and put it through to David, who fired a magnificent shot over the keeper. With five minutes to go, Roy Keane also got a knock and the Gaffer turned to me and said, "Choccy, you'd better warm up, just in case." Kiddo and I stared at him, until he began to get visibly annoyed by my lack of response. I thought he was trying to play a joke on me, but he had genuinely forgotten within the space of two minutes that he had used all three substitutes allowed.

This was probably the most enjoyable game for our spectators for weeks. We took the lead against the run of play, after Spurs hit the bar twice in a matter of seconds through Iversen and Sinton. Our opener was ecstatically greeted by Brian Kidd, because the run that goalscorer Solskjaer made was a move we'd been working on in training. Kiddo wasn't bothered that we had taken the lead; all he wanted to do was point out that it was the move he'd worked on. Our win was crucial, as all our nearest rivals had either drawn or lost the day before. While Kiddo banged on for a few hours, I basked in the reward, eventually, of virtue. We'd not won a game away from home on a Sunday on which I'd been to Mass, apart from the semi final of the Cup last year. I'd almost talked myself into not going to church in order to secure a win.

David May was an unexpected participant in this match. He was booked in for a hernia operation, which had been timed to allow him to make a full recovery for the resumption of the Champions' League games. Unfortunately, the surgeon was taken ill for about the first time in twenty years, so Maysie's operation was cancelled. David has been suffering from two things for the past few weeks: pain from his injury, which made him desperate for the final whistle; and mystification about my latest nickname for him. In an interview, he professed himself to be an admirer of my sense of humour (well, that makes one), but said he was puzzled by my constantly calling him "Sick Boy". He has not seen *Trainspotting*. What did he think I meant?

Following the Spurs match, the Gaffer and Becks stayed up in London for the Sky Sports Awards. None of the rest of the team knew anything about it until David asked me whether I thought he ought to wear formal or more casual attire. Afterwards, the Gaffer told us it was a rowdy and tacky affair. The Manchester United contingent were alternately propositioned by the female guests and barracked by the inebriated audience. Alex Ferguson didn't win the Manager of the Year award, which went to Joe Kinnear. It made me wonder how the voting was organized, as no one else but Alex should have bothered turning up.

In midweek, the Reserves picked up their bid to retain their Pontin's League title against Sheffield Wednesday at Gigg Lane. Ben Thornley scored an excellent goal in our 3–0 win.

While I was driving back from training, I heard Kenny Dalglish being interviewed about his appointment as Newcastle manager. I am a great admirer of his dry sense of humour. One wonderful interchange was a perfect example of the pointless question which appears perfectly acceptable from the interviewer's perspective. Kenny had heard the news of Kevin Keegan's resignation while he was driving to the funeral of a respected Scottish journalist. The interviewer asked, "When you heard the announcement, did you think that you would be offered the job?"

Brief pause. "No." (As if he'd think, "Great, that's brilliant, the job's mine then.")

"When they offered you the job, was there any hesitation or doubt on your part that you would take the post?"

"It took me less time to say yes than it took you to ask that question."

The interviewer then moved on to the last-minute defeat of Newcastle by Southampton.

"When that ball came out to Le Tissier, did you know he would score a goal like that?"

"Well, I knew it was Le Tissier, but no, I didn't expect him to score."

We've got more of that to look forward to, hopefully. He was a great player and has had a tremendous career as a manager. I admire what Kevin Keegan has done, too. If he wanted to resign before the stress of the job did something drastic to him, then he's shown an enormous amount of courage in leaving when he did, rather than holding on.

On Tuesday we had a relatively rare event at Old Trafford, having our picture taken in a new strip. It is blue and bears a very strong resemblance to the Glasgow Rangers' strip, a fact I find very disorientating, though (to add to the confusion) the goalie's colours could be worn by Celtic's custodian.

Our next game was against Coventry on 18 January at Highfield Road, which has some of the strangest dressing rooms in the Premier League. The pegs for your kit are so high up on the wall that you have to stand on the benches to reach them – except for Pally, who can just about get to them from the floor. Either the area is prone to flooding or they were put up by someone very tall. I have a six foot eight brother-in-law, who put a mirror up in his bathroom that no one else can use unless they have a step ladder handy.

In the first half Coventry frustrated us with grim resistance. They could have gone ahead five minutes after half-time, when the very promising Coventry signing Darren Huckerby stumbled after a foul by Gary Neville. The Coventry players screamed for a penalty, but the incident was outside the box. Giggs then fluked a right-foot curler from twenty yards out into the top corner of their net, after winning a challenge aginst Telfer. It was Ryan's first goal for four months – a surprising statistic as his performances have been of a very high quality. Both sides were affected by injury, and Coventry had lost Dion Dublin, one of their most influential players, through suspension. But we seemed to cope with it better and dominated the second half, playing probably some of our best football of the season. Solskjaer put the final result beyond doubt near the end, with a shot which went in off Ogrizovic.

The next Wednesday, we followed up our draw against Wimbledon in the Cup by travelling back down to Selhurst Park to take three vital points in the rain. Once again, changes had been made to the team as key players had come back to fitness, and we were still without David May. We had had long discussions about how we should counter Wimbledon's strengths at set pieces, particularly corners. They duly took the lead with the second ball from a corner – so much for our attention to the team talk. Perhaps the Gaffer's suspicions are warranted. We came back really well and pieced together some good football. United bombarded the Wimbledon goal and hit the woodwork three times, but in the second half Perry scored against the run of play. Giggs equalized with a flicked, back header from a Beckham corner and the winner was poached by Andy Cole after Neil Sullivan saved well from Solskjaer but then couldn't hold on to the ball. The win took us to the top of the Premier League table.

Southampton's visit to Old Trafford at the beginning of February attracted much attention after they had beaten us by so large a margin at the end of 1996. Most reporters seemed to hope that they would be able to repeat their feat of putting six past us. The Saints had had a very bad result in their previous fixture, when they were beaten by Stockport in the FA Cup. But they came out fighting in this match and didn't just try to defend away from home. We thought they would either play Berkovic or Le Tissier, but in the end both players were included and their attacking formation could have paid dividends. Ostenstadt exploited a defensive muddle to put them into the lead. We came close to going two goals down before we got on the scoresheet ourselves. Van Gobbel was through and muffed his shot, but soon after that, in the tenth minute, they scored. It was Pally who brought us level, in his first game back after a few weeks out with injuries. He trapped a ball in the area – well, to be more accurate he leaned forward and it came off his chest and bounced forward – and for some reason the Southampton defenders couldn't seem to pick it up to clear it. The whole incident seemed to be in slow motion from where I was watching. Pally ran forward to get to the ball, stretched out one of his long legs and put a strike into the top corner. It was as though he was the only one who knew what was happening. Eric finally scored the winner after eighty minutes with a fantastic shot which he had to stretch for, and the ball went through their newish goalkeeper. It was yet another three points.

Middlesbrough's success in the Cup competitions meant their League fixture with us was postponed a couple of times. The enforced break did us no harm; the team put in a tremendous performance at Highbury, when play resumed on 19 February. However, the Gaffer and Kiddo were getting very concerned about a potential fixture problem later on in the season if we progressed in the Champions' League. Some of the players had been given a run out the Saturday before the Arsenal match, much to the surprise of Wrexham's A team. We hadn't played for a while so the manager was looking for a game for us, and this was the chosen fixture. When the young lads of Wrexham came out to warm up, May, Cruyff, Thornley, Casper, Butt (and someone who looked like their Dad) were already there. They just stood and stared for a while. We beat them 7–0 and I managed to put away a header. The United A team were still second in their league after that victory, despite the fact that they had also beaten Crewe 10–0. I also played in the return fixture against Forest Reserves at Gigg Lane. The weather was terrible: stormy with torrential rain and high winds. But no amount of rain dancing by myself secured a postponement and we won 4–0.

For the Premiership encounters at Highbury and Stamford Bridge, which took place on the Wednesday and the Saturday, we headed south on Tuesday and stayed down in London for the whole week. It was the professional thing to do, but I can't say that everyone was happy. We had to understand that being rested and not disrupted by continuous travelling was the important thing. These were two difficult games for us which might have had a considerable bearing on the Championship if we had lost both, but, as it transpired, we came away with four points.

Eric was suspended, so against Arsenal we had the speed and thrust up front of what the papers delight in calling a "double strike force", also known as Andy Cole and Ole Gunnar Solskjaer. I thought it was one of our best games of the season, and Arsenal's revival in the second half made it great entertainment.

The match couldn't have gone any better and we were 2–0 up at half-time with contributions from each of our twin strikers. But the quiet tie against Arsenal that I'm convinced is just around the corner was not to be. Something happened in this match that I have never seen before:

the ball burst. Peter came rushing out of his goal again – why I don't know, but at the moment it seems to be what he does – and he and Ian Wright both made contact at the same time. Pally went to kick the deflated ball clear, without noticing that it had gone down. He could have injured himself as he put all his effort into launching it down the park, and it was like booting a rice pudding.

Against teams of the quality of Arsenal, you know you aren't going to dominate the entire match. They really came back at us in the second half. Tony Adams had been forced to go off before the break, and Arsenal changed their system. Despite their improvement Arsenal still created relatively few chances. The goal they scored was partly down to a bit of misfortune for Denis Irwin when, as the cross came over into our box, it caught the Irishman's studs and sat up perfectly for Bergkamp. I say partly because of misfortune, because the Dutchman took the chance with considerable skill to volley it into our net with power and precision.

And then there was the post-match entertainment. Wright's earlier challenge on our goalkeeper had looked dangerous from where I was standing at the side of the pitch next to the referee's assistant. Martin Bodenham, who generally did an excellent job of refereeing throughout the match, decided after consultation with the said assistant that there was nothing to be done about their striker's challenge. Following the obligatory close-range shouting and finger jabbing, things appeared to have settled down and Ian Wright should have gone on to equalize after that. In the last five minutes of the game I devised a plan to go and walk off the pitch with Schmeichel, so that if anything else should happen or something should be said and I was called into action as PFA rep, I would be an expert witness. I can't seem to hold a thought in my head longer than five minutes these days and I completely forgot about this worthy intention as I went over to shake hands with our opponents' staff and applaud our fans for their magnificent vocal support throughout the game. Because of this, rather uselessly, I only caught the very tail end of the aggravation.

A few days later, the *Mirror* described me as acting as a representative in crisis negotiations between the PFA and Peter. This was complete nonsense. Giving Gordon Taylor Peter's phone number because he didn't have it hardly qualifies you as a go-between, does it? I suppose I could have talked to Peter, but we would have had to have been standing at opposite ends of the pitch as he was not very happy at all. A news item on Danish television which suggested he could be imprisoned for an offence which he strenuously denied had upset his relatives in his home country and he was very angry about it. In the view of the PFA, which has launched its own anti-racism campaign, here were two of our high-profile members involved in an allegedly racist incident. If it could have been sorted out by the two men getting together, face-to-face, then it would have been so much better for everyone concerned. I would have thought that was possible, but I didn't have the same kind of personal involvement and my own pride was not at stake. It was no surprise when the Crown Prosecution Service dropped the case later; that was always likely, given the lack of evidence.

The *Mirror* also had a small snippet about how much I wanted to stay at United, even though I could make a small fortune by moving elsewhere when my contract expires. Some of the other players had pointed this out to me in what might be termed a satirical manner, much to my confusion. When, I asked myself, did I give this interview to the *Mirror*? And who are these clubs making their multi-million pound offers? Suddenly all became clear. I had spoken to Piccadilly Radio, and remembered saying that if you asked anyone who had left the club what they thought about going, they'd all say that they missed playing at United. I also said I had no burning desire to leave. As for the rest, there seemed to have been a little journalistic invention – a fact which I pointed out to the paper on the telephone next day.

This week I was asked if I would like to make a video diary along the lines of my literary efforts for the BBC. I declined, as there is enough invasion of privacy in players' lives as it is, and "Choccy's Diary" is also very much about my family life. It wouldn't be right to do something which might make the children's lives a misery at school. The team are no strangers to the handycam, having participated in "The Captain's Log" (a supposedly "candid" video diary of the 1993/94 season) and its imaginatively titled follow-up, "Captain's Log II". The first one was all right, but by the second one we had all had enough and it showed in the final product, particularly as we won nothing at all that season and it ended on a funereal note. We all make regular appearances on the Manchester United Video Magazine, which is produced every three months or so. It's a good product and because of that the players are happy to participate. I have demonstrated my culinary *pièce de resistance*, tagliatelle alla carbonara, and was very surprised not to receive offers for my own cookery programme. I suppose that carbonara and ocean pie wouldn't sustain a whole series, no matter how much panache went into their creation. The carbonara is a huge hit in my own household and Siobhan would be happy for me to cook it most evenings.

The second leg of our London two-parter was at Stamford Bridge. And what a surprise, I got a game. We had quite a pleasant stay at Burnham Beeches. We trained at Bisham Abbey, where the England team train, and we drove round and round the area trying to get back to our hotel, but always seemed to end up at a sign which read "Burnham Beeches, two and a half miles". Signpost spinning is a local sport, it transpired. Finally our driver swallowed his pride and decided to ask someone the way. On the Thursday evening, ten or eleven of us went to the cinema. Ken Merrett, the club secretary was in charge of getting the tickets, because who knows what terrible scrapes ten grown men would get into if they had to purchase their own. When we all trooped in, heads snapped round as Eric was instantly identified. The manager waved at the refreshment counter and boomed, "You can have anything you want, free, if you don't mind signing some autographs!" Sad to say, it was an offer that left us unmoved. All the young lads who would have wolfed down the sweeties had opted to stay behind at the hotel. After accepting a solitary bag of Maltesers for the sake of politeness, we went in to see *Fierce Creatures*. As the adverts and previews played, a woman sitting in front of us turned round and said, very politely, "Excuse me, I know this is a silly question, but what are you all doing here?" Unfortunately, she asked me.

"Well," I grinned, "It's because we've heard that this is the best cinema in the whole of Britain."

"OK." She turned back round. "I knew it was a silly question."

Time in the hotel gave me an opportunity to catch up with my writing of the Diary. It's not an easy job, trying to think up something to say about each day which neither reveals our secrets nor is offensive to the tender flowers we have here, yet is still entertaining for the readers of the magazine. Karel's English must be improving too. He has been specifically assigned as my roomie for that purpose, and I was congratulating myself on the rapid advances he had made when I heard him laughing heartily at an un-subtitled film on the television. However, it turned out to be Philadelphia.

Chelsea kicked off the game at three o'clock on Saturday, but we waited until three minutes past, and by then we were a goal down. Zola confirmed the Gaffer's description of him as "a tricky little b*****" by going round both Denis and Pally to score. Denis slipped and then Pally did likewise, basically making up Zola's mind for him to try a shot. I couldn't believe it. I think we sorted our tactics out after that, as we dominated the second half as they had done in the first. We were happy to have come away with a point (won by another of the trademark screaming long-range shots perfected by David Beckham), but maybe we could have won the game. I had a chance to score with a header. As I rose to meet the ball, I had a wonderful mental picture of it flying into the net, but the reality didn't match up. I was punched in the head by the goalkeeper. I jumped up and was whacked as he thrust his fist at the ball. My granite Airdrie skull protected me from any serious damage, but a little while later the keeper had to have treatment to a shoulder injury sustained while attempting to knock the living daylights out of me and then had to leave the pitch. Afterwards Kiddo told me that as their substitute goalie was getting warmed up on the sidelines, prancing around in his multi-coloured gear, he had remarked drily, "Now I wonder who is coming off?" "The goalkeeper!" Eric cried out helpfully, anxious to ease our coach's perplexity. As the tale unfolded I knew that this had to go into the Diary. Eric reached into his pocket to pull out a wedge of money.

"Choccy," he pleaded desperately, "Name your price to keep it out!"

"No, Eric," I told the king of cool, "I cannot be bought. I merely serve the interests of my public."

We were allowed fish and chips on the way home.

Another shopping story. A friend told me he'd watched a series about shopping on the television, and advanced a theory that the reason I found shopping so therapeutic was because I went into a trance state while prowling the aisles. I refute this: I am a very focused shopper. I know exactly what I want and the only item I spend any time browsing over is wine. But my shopping nirvana seems to be turning into a private hell after another example of my interference with other people's shopping. On a recent outing, I was idling over the bottles, casually eavesdropping on a bizarre conversation the couple next to me were having, when I finished my selection, dropped two bottles into my trolley and sped off towards the checkout with the fixed purpose of someone who had accomplished his mission. The man I'd been listening to came running after me, red-faced, and I thought, "Someone else who's got something about football they've just got to tell me. Never mind, let's get it over with." And I turned to face him.

"Can I have my trolley back?" he spluttered indignantly. Sure enough, I'd walked off with his shopping. You can imagine him going home and complaining that you can't go into a supermarket nowadays without some minor celebrity brazenly waltzing off with your goods.

9

Future perfect

"Absolutely no idea, Gaffer!"

In mid-February came a week made free by international fixtures, during a "quiet" part of the season before the European campaign resumed. I decided to begin preparations for whatever my future might be when I stop playing. This involved going down to the most basic level of the FA coaching qualifications, the preliminary certificate. This qualifies you to coach people up to the age of sixteen. Though you don't necessarily require the badges to become a coach, things are changing fast from the days when all you seemed to need was the ability to shout very loudly for prolonged periods, though obviously this is still a major requirement. I decided it was far better to do my studying while I was still actively involved in playing. The preliminary certificate is also now part of the elementary training of the second year YTS lads, and I discovered that the quickest way to gain the award is to tag along at the back of a group of seventeen-year-olds. I was fortunate that some of the YTS students from Manchester City, Bury and Rochdale who had missed the course the first time round were doing a crash course over three days. It was with some trepidation that I went back to school, nearly twice the age of everyone there except the teachers.

The course I enrolled on is run by the PFA, whose small coaching department has been taken over by Andy Welsh from Paul Power, who is now with Manchester City. There are practical sessions, accompanied by lectures at Maine Road on topics such as nutrition and CPR (Cardio Pulmonary Resuscitation). There I received not the first lecture I've ever had from a referee, but certainly the longest, on Laws of the Game. We began with the multiple choice ref's exam, during which my mind went spectacularly blank for two of the questions, and followed it with some first aid. The CPR dummies provided endless amusement for the less mature among us.

We also had homework to do. One of the exercises involved watching a particular player for the duration of a game and tracing his movements, ticking them off on a worksheet to show that you can interpret what is happening throughout the match. The course work book was easy to follow but I had one enormous problem with it. On Tuesday night, after my first day's study, I climbed wearily into bed with my book and turned to Module One: Attitudes and Ethics, a very worthy set of topics indeed. Within a few minutes of beginning my earnest perusal, I was demonstrating the techniques of lying with my cheek stuck to the page and snoring professionally.

The next day was a practical session. The usual extreme weather conditions prevailed; the rain belted down every day and a high wind whipped around Platt Lane, City's training ground. We used the Astro-turf surface there and the balls just kept blowing away. We ran through every single basic topic for a professional footballer, from long passing, short passing, running with the ball, dribbling, small-sided games, defensive play and shooting to goalkeeping. After a quick lunch it was back to Maine Road for more seminars. When I'd gone there the day before, in my Manchester United training kit, the place had been deserted and I'd been able to sneak in unobserved. But on Wednesday there were queues around the ground for tickets for City's FA Cup game against Middlesbrough. I had to walk 100 yards to the main entrance, and any hopes of remaining inconspicuous were soon dashed. They spotted me immediately. Someone had to shout out something: "Hey, McClair, I hope you've not come to collect some free tickets, you *******!" A number of witty ripostes sprang to mind instantly ("No, I've just won a tenner on the lottery and I've come to buy the club"), but I was mindful that my car was parked not very far away. I opted for maintaining what I hoped was a dignified yet enigmatic silence, but probably looked as though I was keeping my head down to avoid more graphic verbal abuse.

By the time I reached home and put the kids to bed, it had been another very long day, but there was still my swotting to do. It was with the best of intentions that I began module two, "Learning strategies and coaching styles", propped up on my pillow. I read the first page four times trying to absorb it before nodding off.

The third day involved an initial assessment of practical skills. Despite having a reasonably successful career as a player and being a great deal older than anyone else – or perhaps because of that – I was very, very nervous when I had to demonstrate the first of my three topics. The young lads who were my fellow students had been tremendous fun but I was still worried that I would make a fool of myself in front of them. When I got through the technique of turning with the ball with some success, I was very relieved.

Some of the YTS lads there with me may end up as coaches, but the main reason for them to take the certificate is that some knowledge of nutrition, fitness and some avoidable injuries (Module Four: Football fitness; Module Five: Overuse Injuries, Child Protection; Module Seven: "Football Food One") will be helpful to them in looking after their own bodies as professionals. As we filled out our worksheets it struck me that I may know what protein is, and that there is absolutely none at all in lager, but not everybody will be so well-informed – especially if your education was seriously disrupted since the age of twelve by the demands of schoolboy football.

The next stage for me was to complete sixteen hours of coaching, which I nearly managed to finish before the demands of the season pre-occupied me again. I still had three more topics to do but they'd have to wait until the start of the next season. I intend to progress to the UEFA B licence, a residential course at Lilleshall. The biggest problem will be fitting in the coaching hours, as you need a cross-section of children and adults. Perhaps there's a pub team out there which will let me practice on them. Though you've been mastering the skills required to play football throughout your career, the trick is to learn how to organize training exercises to put them over to others in a simple yet entertaining way. You have to see where someone is going wrong and put over how they can correct it, and it's not as easy as you may think to do either. The best way, of course, is to be able to demonstrate it yourself. Not that there is a right way or a wrong way to do things in football, so hopefully in coaching there is scope for imagination. But these certificates are only the very beginning. It's an obvious point, but you can only learn coaching by doing it and for some it can be a long and bitter apprenticeship.

When I stop playing professionally I'd rather coach than go into the business or administrative side of the game if I have the chance, because I think I'll always feel a need to play football at some level. I can't conceive of doing without it. I can't imagine not being out on the field every day with players, and a coach's job seems far more attractive than being stuck in an office by a telephone. I am sure that the bigger clubs are close to the point of moving over to the continental model, with a coach who trains and picks the teams and a general manager who looks after the organization, books hotels, flights and sees to the other minutiae. There are rumours from time to time that I am being groomed to be manager here – rumours that I do nothing to dampen and everything to encourage. In my dreams, eh?

Careers for ex-footballers could be changing very quickly in other respects. There are many employment opportunities available in football, but they are there precisely because there are a great many full-time clubs. Part of the reason players should have a political involvement in the game through the PFA is to safeguard the continued existence of every football club. It's to the advantage of professionals to keep as many options open as possible. We have more full-time footballers than anywhere else in the world; the structure of our game, with all its divisions, provides somewhere to start out and gain coaching and management experience for most of them who want to.

Of course, if I aspire to becoming a coach eventually, I could do worse than model myself on the man from Collyhurst himself, Brian Kidd. He has two unique coaching talents which he uses to great effect. His main method of encouraging us to greater efforts in training is to be "economical with the truth". If we moan about the amount of running we're doing pre-season, he'll announce, "Running! This isn't running!" There's no advantage to be gained from pointing out to him that putting one leg in front of the other one at speed would fit most definitions of running, because he's convinced that whatever he says is correct. Then he'll say, "That's your running finished with now, lads, it's over for the season!" A week later we'll be doing something that I could swear was running, but who am I to contradict him?

His other trick is one he has played on everyone here. Occasionally, when they've needed time to do something urgently, players have asked him if they can take a day off. "You can have Monday off, no problem!" is his usual answer. Then you'll return on Tuesday and go into the coach's room where the Gaffer will look at you sternly and Kiddo will ask, "Oh, there you are, did you enjoy your holiday, then?" A couple of weeks ago, Eric had a car problem. Kiddo said, as usual, "Take Monday off, Tuesday if you need it." On the Monday, I just happened to be in the coaching room when the Gaffer wandered in from his own room next door, where he had begun to feel a bit lonely.

"Where's Eric got to today?" he queried testily.

"Absolutely no idea, Gaffer," replied Kiddo, looking solemn.

Though it may not sound like it, Kiddo is the buffer between the manager and the players and the players and the manager. He structures the first-team training after discussion with the Gaffer. He draws up a plan for the whole week's training, though the Gaffer may not always agree with it and want to do something else. His task is to ensure that we are all at that peak of fitness, and to achieve this he is a keen student of training techniques from Europe, particularly Italy and Spain. His belief is that fitness should be achieved through skill work (not through cross-country runs or struggling up sand dunes), and that fitness training and developing football skills should not be seen as two separate exercises. Rather than weight-training, he'll have us shooting for twenty minutes, which works all major muscle groups but improves our play at the same time. He has the gift of making training interesting, constantly changing and varying the exercises, playing keep ball, passing in a 40 x 40 box, eight against eight, two-touch, all sorts of things.

The manager... how can I put it... kind of manipulated him into the job of first team coach just before the European Cup Winners' Cup in 1991, when Archie Knox left to join Rangers. He was asked to take training one day and is still doing it. Another example of the Gaffer's luck – or foresight. He didn't tell Kiddo he wanted him to take on that particular role, it just came about. Kiddo was youth development officer and popular with the players already; he's still the same character as he was then. He is quite happy to join you in a laugh, as long as you also do your work. He enjoys practical jokes along the lines of filling your sock with sugar while you are out training, and other merry pranks.

Brian Kidd is very good indeed at his job, and it's something that he has not learnt overnight. He had a couple of spells in management as well as playing in the USA. It is also obvious that he really enjoys what he does. He takes a justifiable pride in the part he has played in the success of the team over the last six years. If something that he's been working on comes off in a game, he is absolutely thrilled. Kiddo is a very different person from the Gaffer and the contrast between them makes them a very strong partnership. What they do both share is an enormous ambition, which drives them on to achieve even more success. That's not to say that Brian Kidd is desperate for the Gaffer's job, as some people have made out; I don't think that's the case. It seems to me, as far as I can judge, that he's much more comfortable coaching – and he has been a manager before, though in very different circumstances, it's true.

It has been argued that he provides a much-needed, light-hearted counterpoint to what is mistakenly perceived to be the Gaffer's dourness. I remember when we failed to win the title in 1991/92, much nonsense was written about how Alex Ferguson's tension had communicated itself to the team so that they stuttered in the run-up. That is a complete misreading of the Gaffer's character. He may come across in a particular way in interviews, as a man who doesn't have the greatest sense of humour. In fact, he is a man who loves to laugh and joke, albeit in a different style from Brian Kidd. You wouldn't take any liberties with either of them and they are always treated with the utmost respect by players.

Another misapprehension is that Kiddo is the calmer of the two, and there have been some well-publicized occasions where he appears to have restrained a furious Gaffer from committing an indiscretion but Kiddo is just as volatile. Everyone remembers his impromptu celebration in 1993 when Steve Bruce headed the extra-time winner against Sheffield Wednesday. At Anfield this season, the Gaffer wasn't on the bench at the start of the game but in the stands. I was sitting next to Kiddo, who was in a state of extreme agitation from the moment the whistle went. After the first few minutes I had to say to him, "Look, will you just calm down and stop shouting, there's eighty-six minutes to go!" Everyone gets worked up during a match, but Kiddo lost it right from the word go that day.

Neither he nor the manager hold back if they have something they think should be said. Whether it's about team selection, coaching or a player's behaviour, Brian Kidd will come straight out with what he believes, even if it is not what the Gaffer wants to hear. But (contrary again to rumour) they don't fall out with each other. The manager's attitude on was spelled out to me just the other day when he observed, "I've never fallen out with a coach or a player. But plenty of them have fallen out with me!"

The planned new training complex, which will move us away from the Cliff in Salford to Carrington Moss, is a project very dear to Kiddo's heart. He feels it is essential if United is going to maintain its position and have the chance to win European honours. It will allow him and his successors to give us the best possible preparation. He's been very influenced by the models used by the top Italian and Spanish clubs, an admiration which necessitates trips abroad to hot countries to pay homage and pick up tips and a tan. He is very disappointed that it appears very likely that the planning permission for the new site won't allow for residential use. This means that it won't be possible to create a complete Italian-style unit which would radically change the way we train at present. Ideally, each player would have a room of his own which would be pretty spartan, but comfortable, with a bed, TV and somewhere to hang clothes. He would be expected to stay overnight before home games or where there were a number of games in succession – over Easter, Christmas or at the end of the season. This wouldn't be very popular with players or their families, just as it isn't particularly liked by Italian footballers, but it would be accepted if it were part of the deal to play for a club as big as United.

Although I'd no date fixed for it yet, my testimonial match programme was being prepared and friends and former colleagues were approached to provide some comments about me. Two of them, Andy Roxburgh and Archie Knox, seemed to suggest that I am less than enthusiastic when it comes to the business of training. Archie's words were, "He is the type of player that you can rely upon to do his job well... It's just a pity I cannot say the same about his training." Andy Roxburgh was equally direct: "It became clear that the real Brian McClair was not to be found on the training pitch: he only flowered in the often chaotic turbulent 'battlefield' of competition." If I take you through the typical training day at Old Trafford at the time when we were preparing for the most testing part of the season, perhaps I can illuminate the reasons why this commonly echoed belief about myself and training is a misconception.

I am usually one of the first players to present myself for training at the Cliff. Even Archie remembered this in his eulogy for the testimonial programme. "True, he always presented himself on time," he wrote, before going on to suggest that this in itself was not necessarily a virtue.

It takes me about half an hour to drive from the house, but it could be longer depending on the weather. When it rains in Manchester it's such a surprise that everyone slows down to look. I have my own parking space at the Cliff, an innovation introduced a few years back since more and more of the young players have their own cars. There was endless confusion and delay as people practised the time-honoured art of parking as close to the buildings as they could. The senior players are now closest to the door, forwards on one side and defenders on the other. Despite being the longest-serving player, I do not have the coveted spot closest to the entrance. Sparky Hughes is a month older than me and he had that honour until he left, then his space was usurped by Peter Schmeichel. Once Peter decided he was going to have it, who was I to argue with his great big Mercedes? I can walk another six feet or so, even if he does have much longer legs than I do.

Waiting for you as you come in are usually a small line of apprentices who have been given the job of getting strips, gloves, hats, balls, posters, calenders – piles of the stuff – signed by the players. Wherever you go in this club, as I've said before, the merchandise follows, but it only takes a few minutes and is usually for good causes. Sometimes the coaches will waylay you for the same purpose. The next stop is the first-team dressing room, which I'm used to having to myself for a while to change before heading upstairs for a bite to eat for breakfast. Sometimes I've already eaten at home, but breakfast at the Cliff is one of my favourite experiences. Teresa, who is in charge of preparing the food, begins cooking at some unearthly hour like four in the morning, so much of what will be dished up for lunch is already prepared. This means you can select some bizarre mixtures for your first meal of the day. I've had a peas and mince sandwich, a lasagne sandwich and a chop before now, but I generally restrain myself and go for a piece or toast and jam or a roll and cheese. It's a bit like a school canteen and it performs the same invaluable function: making sure that the young apprentices come in and actually eat breakfast, rather than a bar of chocolate and a bag of crisps, and that they sit down to one, well-balanced meal a day (as

rian Kidd enjoys practical jokes along the lines of filling your socks with sugar while are training and other merry pranks."

21 December 1996, Old Trafford: Manchester United 5, Sunderland 0. "I made a goal for Eric. No skill was required; he couldn't miss. Actually, he made the task look as difficult as possible."

19 February 1997, Highbury: Arsenal 1, Manchester United 2. "One day we will play against Arsenal and absolutely nothing controversial will happen."

Demonstrating *tagliatelli alla carbonara* for the Manchester United video magazine.

The Golden Boot for forty-one goals for Celtic in the 1986/87 season.

5 March 1997, Old Trafford: Manchester United 4, FC Porto 0. "I get along with Alex Ferguson – if I didn't, he would have got rid of me long ago because of the things I've said to his face – but rumours about me being his son are unfounded."

"A record of thirty caps
and two goals has a
certain symmetry to it...
And now my children
believe they're English."

"I was asked to put myself forward for the PFA Management Committee by my
friend Pat Nevin, the current chairman of the English Association."

"I was Billy McNeill's last signing for Celtic before he left to manage Aston Villa. One fan was quoted as saying that I would never score any goals for the club and my 'derisory' tranfer fee was considered a waste of money. I 'only' scored 120 in my four years as a Celt, mind."

Below: the winning goal against Liverpool at Anfield, en route to the first Championship, in 1993.

European Cup Winners' Cup, 1990/91, Old Trafford: Manchester United 1, Montpellier 1. "We began by taking an early lead when I thumped home a shot from Lee Sharpe's cross."

European Cup Winners' Cup final, 1990/91, Rotterdam: Manchester United 2, Barcelona 1. "Barcelona were an excellent team and full of stars, but we beat them on the night."

1992 Rumbelows Cup winner: "Brian! Don't put on any more hats, you just look stupid!"

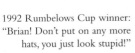

"I wonder if the young players here can really appreciate how good it is to win a Championship when they've not reached a nadir like we did in 1989/90?"

"I do moan in training: if I do have a speciality, I think this could be it."

recommended in my worksheet, Football Food One). We older men can also graze around there if we want to, before and after training.

Once satisfied, my leisurely start to training would not be complete without the intellectual nourishment provided over tea and coffee back in the dressing room, where the players and others who have since arrived gather to discuss whatever has caught their eye in the papers: interest rates, burning political issues, the essential tragedy of the human condition – and cars and women. If you have picked up an injury, how-ever, your day will have a different start as you have to report to the physio's room as quickly as possible.

Punctuality is not so easy for some as it is for others, and there is a system of fining for persistent lateness for all aspects of training. If you are not in the building for treatment at ten o'clock, your misdemeanour will be chalked up on the physio's board. There are other things you can be penalized for. For example, you're not allowed to take any news-papers or books into physio – in fact, you're not allowed to enjoy your-self at all when you're there. Once I suggested that they might put a TV on the wall or something, but was told in no uncertain terms, "You're here because you're not fit to play, not to have a good time!" I suppose it's a bit like army medical parade. The belief is that if the physio's room was a welcoming place, some players might abuse it and sit there reading and relaxing for an hour or so until they were chucked out as malingerers. How cynical. Anyone would think footballers are constantly prone to behaving like children. You have to be there on time for your treatment, or to say that there's something amiss. By 10.15, the physios are expected in the coaches' room with a list of players ready to go back into training after injury, as well as the ones who won't be able to train today.

Training proper is a short distance away at Littleton Road, which causes some problems because no one wants to take their car. Muddy boots and kit on the way back to the Cliff can make a terrible mess of the inside of your car, so there is much jockeying and horse-trading between players to force someone to give them a lift. In the temples to cleanliness that are the young players' expensive motors, a set of stud prints would cause mayhem. If you're not at Littleton Road for 10.30 you'll be fined again, though by this time in the season there has been a slight erosion of standards and it creeps ever closer to 10.35. Kiddo keeps tabs and if you have problems organizing yourself, the manager will know and will speak to you about it. Not that I have had this problem as I am pathologically incapable of being late. Enormous pangs of guilt assail me even at the thought of it, and the one or two times it has happened have all been Pally's fault. Nobody else here seems to share my particular punctuality problem. The fines set are standard across football and have been agreed by various bodies. Guidelines are given out based upon percentages of salaries. The fines are cumulative. It's funny how people are creatures of habit and how they stick to set patterns. There's me always early, and others who scrape in at the last minute so regularly that you can set your watch by them.

We train for one and a half hours, from 10.30 to 12.00. The session always beginning with a warm-up taken by Kiddo. He has some little, soft leather balls for keepy-uppy, we may run in and out of poles and do some forward rolls — of which he is inordinately fond and likes to incorporate wherever he can. He claims that they have a serious purpose, but I think that he probably puts them in because no one can do them properly and he enjoys watching our various levels of incompetence. As I've mentioned, we have a mixture of fitness and skills training with the emphasis on developing our techniques. Today we worked on possession in a grid, with four players versus four, one touch, before finishing up with eight against eight in a larger area with some heading. We always finish with a game with reduced numbers on a small pitch. And as for my training style, I refute utterly the imputation that I am a poor trainer. I certainly get through the work. It's just that I manage to give my all in a way that suggests I'm not exactly killing myself, if you understand what I mean. I've never been one for showing off. I do moan in training; if I have a speciality, I think this could be it. But we all do; getting irritated and having little tiffs with each other when a stray boot barks your shins is all part of it. Some days training is enjoyable; most days it's not. I suppose it depends on your biorhythms.

We certainly have no worries about the level of fitness Brian Kidd brings us up to. None of us has ever contemplated faxing off to Italy for our own private schedule. Most of what Kiddo takes us through comes from Italy anyway. It must be pretty tricky doing your own training, crossing to yourself, passing to yourself, saving your own shots. I couldn't do it in my own street; there'd be the ever-present danger of Pally running you over. My earlier mention of sand dunes makes me think of other training regimes I have known, and one in particular. Jock Wallace once took the Motherwell squad to the beach at Gullane. As a boy, reading the back pages of my dad's *Daily Express*, I'd read about how Rangers were going training there and always believed it was in France. Actually it's on the east coast of Scotland, along the Firth of Forth between Musselburgh and North Berwick.

On that memorable day we began by running back and forward along the beach to the sand dunes, and I can remember thinking, foolishly, that it wasn't bad at all. However, this was only the warm-up. Even so one of our number was sick at this point. "Aye, thas right laddie, feed tha seagulls," Jock observed, with grim satisfaction. The real pain began when we had to run up and down the dunes. We came to the appropriately named "Murder Hill" and it crossed my mind as I looked at the gradient that this was a joke. It wasn't. We had to run up and down it. My brain has, in the interests of mercy, blotted out just how many times we had to do it. One refinement that the Inquisition would have envied was the part where we ran up to the top, ran part of the way back down and then turned to essay the steepest part again. Your arms were pumping like pistons but you made no progress in the heavy sand. We finished by running down and straight into that part of the Arctic Ocean known as the North Sea.

We went to have a bite to eat afterwards, but no one was interested. I tried lifting my fork to my mouth but my arms wouldn't respond to the messages from my brain. Our one thought was to get back home and into our beds. Surprisingly, I managed all the ordeals so carefully prepared for us, but going back on the bus I was completely wiped out with no strength left anywhere. Jock was pleased. "Aye," he mused, "That was really gud. We'll come back halfway through the season jist tae test yir fitness!" I looked at him in disbelief. All the way through that season, I was dreading the announcement that we were going back to the dunes.

When Jock went to manage Leicester (the Midlands are the furthest you can be away from the sea in Britain), he had to, in a manner of speaking, bring the dunes to him. A dune was constructed for training purposes out of builders' sand. And it worked, because twenty years later, this season, Leicester would win the Coca-Cola Cup. I watched *The Hill* starring Sean Connery a few weeks ago, and as the sadistic prison guard forced the men up the feature mentioned in the title I thought, "I could do that. In fact, I have done it."

To return to our own training, some players do like to stay out longer, especially if we have been practicising shooting, but the Gaffer does not encourage it. If it goes on too long he'll bang on the window and shout, "Yir fined, get in!" He doesn't want players to train any longer than Brian Kidd has stipulated because the regimes are carefully designed to include all the training you'll need. He'd rather you did less and erred on the side of caution, never forgetting that training is not an end in itself but a preparation for matches. It's back to the Cliff after that, having ruined the interiors of a few cars. We shower, flick each other with wet towels in a hearty, manly way, scrub each others' backs and dress ourselves. I like to hang around for a bit afterwards and have some tea, but others shoot off as quickly as possible. We used to say that Lee Martin (now with Bristol Rovers) had an all-in-one suit that he stepped into and zipped up the front as he was dressed and away so quickly. But no matter how quickly you change to rush off, you cannot easily escape the crowds outside.

A visit to the Cliff has become one of the favourite stations of the pilgrimage to Old Trafford and our public are now always there, waiting for autographs or a glimpse of their heroes. Fans are only locked out on a Friday when we work out our strategy for dealing with the opposition, though people only have to go up the hill opposite or walk down by the river to see in. It attracts all sorts; groups of teenage girls who scream loudly at David Beckham, families who travel hundreds of miles to be there. Sometimes I answer the telephone at the Cliff, pretending to be a steward, and it gives me a glimpse of the miles people are prepared to come. It might be a family from Dorset who are intending to make a day trip and want to know when we'll be there. In school holidays it is absolutely packed and sometimes there are just too many people to stop and sign autographs for, as it can be so dangerous when they all push forward. Generally, we do try to accommodate people and give them what they want and usually the fans are appreciative. I had a lovely letter from a family the other day who thanked me for taking time to chat and sign things for them. I'm not sure that I necessarily understand why they do it, standing in the rain for up to four hours just to see us. Not everyone can get to a match or afford to take their children to the game, so I suppose this is one alternative. But if you are in any sort of a hurry you just have to turn your stereo up loud and attempt not to run anyone over as you leave.

It's better than having nobody coming to see you or, as happened in 1989, coming to give you stick. Once I saw four or five bigs lads who came to discuss the team's diabolical form. They walked in and announced, "What the ***** going on? Where's the manager?"

"He's in there, lads," I gestured helpfully, moving off towards my car, jumping in and driving off.

10

A song for Europe

"That's never gone in, has it?"

The pace of the season, which never really slackened, picked up again as the two month break between the qualifying legs of the Champions' League and the knock-out rounds came to an end. During this time we had established ourselves at the top of the Premier League and March began with Coventry scoring two goals for us to maintain our lead. Not that anyone expected our challenge in Europe to detain us very far into Spring 1997. In the quarter finals our opponents were the Portuguese champions, Porto, who had come top of their qualifying group without losing a game, in contrast to our own three defeats. Commentators at home and abroad predicted we would struggle and be bested by a large margin. The Gaffer's increasing concern at the possible fixture pile-up at the season's end, should we progress further in European competition, was openly derided. A combination of frozen pitches, Middlesbrough's progress in the two domestic Cup competitions and match-free weekends before internationals threatened to force United to play four or so fixtures in the concluding week of the Premier League, as we had done in 1992 with dire consequences. There wouldn't be so much of a problem if and when, as predicted, we were trounced by the Portuguese club. If you were paranoid, you might almost sense a crossing of fingers so that would happen, as it would save much embarrassment in certain quarters.

Wednesday 5 March brought the Old Trafford leg against Porto. It saw us go, I am happy to say, from the semi-ridiculous at Highfield Road to the sublime. This must have been one of the most fluent and commanding of our performances in Europe ever. The fact that we weren't considered capable of it made it even sweeter. With hindsight you could argue that everything that could have gone right for us did. We played Porto at just the right time. Their own form in the Portuguese League had dipped, and they had drawn and lost their last two games. In the match directly preceding their visit to Old Trafford they were defeated by a last-minute penalty and one of their players had been sent off. Porto's chief coach, Antonio Oliveira, was under pressure, and the club was beset by allegations of financial scandal. Their fans had waved huge fake banknotes in the stands in protest. But maybe our 4–0 scoreline was not so much a reflection of the tribulations of our opponents, but the excellence of our own play. We had a slightly shaky start and could easily have been a goal down after the first five minutes. If they had scored then they could have gone on to win the match, but once we had been fortunate enough to survive that early chance thanks to Gary Pallister, United were magnificent.

Porto did manage to have a huge amount of possession throughout, without creating too many clear-cut goal opportunities, but when it came to scoring goals we put everything together. The first goal was hardly a classic, if our two centre backs who were instrumental in giving us the lead will forgive me for saying so. After his intial corner had been cleared, Beckham swung in a powerful cross from the left which Pallister met well, but his header was blocked by the goalkeeper on the line. David May stuck out a leg while falling over in the other direction and knocked the ball past Hilario. The second goal came from a long kick out by Peter. Solskjaer attempted to thread it through for Cantona, but found a Porto defender who, in trying to clear, knocked the ball against his own leg. Eric ran on to the rebound and scored with a strike that the goalkeeper really should have stopped. It didn't go under him but he was slow to get to it.

The scoreline at the end of the first half was beyond our expectations but we matched it in the second half. Looking back, it seems to me that we had an opportunity to increase our lead every time we came forward.

Beckham came very close to making it 3–0, then Eric turned defence into attack by playing a superb ball from our own area down the line. Andy Cole ran with it and drew the defender, then played the cleverest of balls for Ryan Giggs, who was making a run into the penalty area, to shoot hard and low, under the goalkeeper. Once again the Porto goalie should have done better with it, but every part of that goal was a superb piece of football. Though the whole team on the night put on a wonderful collective display, it is impossible not to single out the performance of Ryan, who was electrifying in every aspect. His tackling in midfield was tenacious and he contributed to the breaking up of much of Porto's play. The speed of his breaks forward was breathtaking. Our final goal once again came quickly from a defensive situation. Neville and Johnsen cleared quickly and then Eric turned provider, playing another ball for Andy Cole to run at. The keeper rushed out to stop him and by doing so he made up Andy's mind for him. What I'm saying here is that Hilario did not have a good game at all.

It was a terrific night and the noise made by the crowd was deafening. We also ensured that by not conceding a goal, our first-leg lead was even more commanding.

Following the Porto success, we played a practice match for an Israeli centre half from Malta who was at Old Trafford on trial. The first teamers (with the exception of Roy Keane) took on the "rest". It was with an almost unseemly amount of pleasure that we gave the top men a 7–0 thrashing, and refused to allow the fact that they were all pretty well exhausted dim our enjoyment or sense of achievement in the slightest.

Given the scoreline from the first game, our main concern in the away leg of the quarter finals two weeks later on 19 March turned out not to be the match itself, but outside events. Players could see clearly from the pitch and bench that something was going on, either in the stadium itself or just outside it, but we couldn't find out exactly what it was. Even before the actual incidents which were to fill the papers for the next few days, it was apparent that all was not well. As our fans began to take their places in numbers, prior to the warm-up, we could see that when people were coming in through the steep entrances and exits, they were tumbling down two or three rows, and some were even falling over the seats. We were worried by that, as it looked as if some of them were getting hurt. I went over to talk to a friend of mine whom I had spotted in the crowd. I asked him if there were any problems. He told me that it was pandemonium outside, but he seemed to think it was largely a question of disorganization and that the Portuguese authorities were unable to cope with the large numbers of fans we had brought with us. He didn't feel that there was serious cause for concern, but then he had entered ground relatively early on.

We came out to warm up. By then, Gary Neville had become particularly anxious at the way events were shaping. He wanted to know exactly what was going on outside as rumours had started to filter through. He does get worried at the best of times, as his family travel everywhere to watch himself and Phil play. It wasn't until we came out on to the pitch that we got a clear sense of just how many United fans were in the stadium. It was packed. From a cursory inspection, it appeared that conditions inside the ground were hardly conducive to safety. The section that contained the United fans had some seats in it, but it didn't look as though there would be enough for the numbers that were being packed in. Many of the Porto fans were standing on big concrete steps, with no crush barriers – which seemed incredible, given the regulations that exist to ensure crowd safety now.

Our own journey to the stadium had hardly been relaxing. In order to reach the ground in time through the dense, barely moving traffic, a man had hung out of the door of the accompanying police car, pushing other vehicles which blocked our way off the road. You could call it exciting – well, we've all seen *Speed* – but we were on the edge, some of us literally, by the time the stadium came into view. After that the game didn't live up to the promise of the preliminaries. We can file this one under the heading "professional performance", but it is as important to be able to tie a game up like that as to take a team apart. We knew we couldn't expect things to go as well a second time, especially when

Porto were at home. After an early flourish from which they failed to score, we kept firm control of the match. We were perfectly happy that it ended 0–0 and we were in no real danger of not progressing to the semis. I was more than perfectly happy; to be honest, I was delirious. When you know, as I did, that after a long career of competing in Europe, first with Celtic and then with United, this will be one of the last opportunities to be involved as a player, whether I was needed as sub or not, it was brilliant to think we might go all the way. Adding a Champions' League winners' medal to my collection would round it all off very nicely indeed.

Little did I know that, although I hadn't kicked a ball at all for the ninety minutes, I was to enter the limelight inadvertently thanks to a Portuguese cameraman. I'm told that the pictures that reached home of our post-match celebrations showed me having a joke with Phil Neville. Near the finish, Phil had been through on goal but had not taken the opportunity to shoot when he had a clear scoring chance. I put my hand on his shoulder and spun him round to face the goal, saying, "Would you like to go through that again? Look, I'll go in goal, you come along like you were doing, only this time, shoot!" It's the sort of thing you might do if you thought no one was watching; only it happened to be in front of millions worldwide. Phil was explaining to me what had gone through his mind and why he didn't. Embarrassingly, reporters were agog to find out what I'd said. I claimed I was telling him to wave to his mum and dad. Much more worthy of attention was the tremendous reception the Portuguese fans gave our team at the end as we saluted the crowd, applauding us off the pitch. On a more ominous note, we saw the police dressed in riot gear lining up in front of the United end at the close, but then we were hustled onto the bus to begin our journey back.

It was while we were travelling to the airport that something happened which took the gloss off our triumph. We received a phone call to say that ten fans had been shot at the game and that one was dead. We all thought that nothing was worth the loss of that one life. For fifteen to twenty minutes, until we found out differently, we were very quiet. It turned out that someone had confused reports of trouble at the match with an account of a bank robbery in Porto that evening, where one of the robbers had been shot and killed. But it was some while before we worked out that was the case and until it was cleared up it was a dreadful feeling. Not that we didn't think it was bad enough that plastic bullets had been used on fans who seemed to have only been trying to protect their own safety. Most kinds of things that happen at football grounds you can keep at a distance, but players had friends or family involved, as well as being anxious that fans had weapons used against them. They were definitely shaken.

The pictures in the press next day of fans shot and bleeding don't need any comment from me. It's only right that United fans were exonerated by UEFA of any blame some months later; though they changed their tune for no apparent reason months later, when they reduced Porto's fine to £12,000. It's a great shame that the images of the injuries will be the lasting memory of an evening which seems to have been marked by good relations between both sets of supporters.

On the flight out, the captain invited me into the cabin to answer my comments about air travel and what he took to be the criticism of pilots' abilities in the Diary. There wasn't much I could say, really; I was on his plane, after all. If you are in the cabin you don't notice anything at the time of landing as you are in front of the wheels.

Our progress to the semi finals also meant that we had another essential to consider preparing – the Cup final single. As I look responsible, it seems to be my lot to organize this particular aspect of a footballer's job. Unjustly, I think, I have received criticism for the standard of some of our efforts. Any blame is unjust, because it is traditional for football records to be awful – with one notable exception. Take "Three Lions", for instance. Ian Broudie will have to live that one down for a long time, but it's proof that quality, or rather a distinct lack of it, is no hindrance to a football song's eventual success. The first record that can be held against me was the 1990 Cup song (I can't remember what it was, but it was pretty dire). It sold about five copies. For 1993 I was contacted by a member of Status Quo, who said that his group were interested in doing a record with us. I can't say I'm their biggest fan and they're not everyone's cup of tea, but no one can deny that they've been very successful at what they do. We met Rick Parfitt and Francis Rossi and had a good laugh in making the single, "Come on you Reds". They made things very easy as they were very professional about arranging the production and other technical matters. What can you say about the fact that it went to number one and sold over 400,000 copies? The year after our first double saw us venture into rap, with the usual degree of success which accompanies football players when they attempt that style. It was called "We're gonna do it again!" but we didn't, that season anyway. Despite that, it was still a top ten single. Our last contribution to the genre, "Move, Move, Move" produced by Pete Waterman, was... all right.

Perhaps this time, though, we had the opportunity to make the only listenable Manchester United single of all time. The proposal was for a European Cup final anthem, a collaboration between Joe Strummer (ex-Clash), Shaun Ryder (ex-Happy Mondays, Black Grape and a Manc) and Tim Burgess of the Charlatans; they produced a demo. Even if no one bought it, I believed it would be one to enjoy. I was much more enthusiastic about this than the other musical projects mooted. One was a Christmas ballad, though even someone with as vivid imagination as myself couldn't picture what the squad would sound and look like, straining around the Christmas tree. And as for the suggested LP, three minutes is surely more than enough to inflict on the public. It might have been worth it to see if we could top the 1972 team's abysmal rendition of "Chirpy Chirpy Cheep Cheep", but some things are impossible to follow.

No footballer will ever tell you that they like making these records, but we don't actively dislike doing it. It's all part of the modern professional's life. No matter how much of an idiot it might make you feel, any embarrassment is usually soothed by the cheque. I remember Bryan Robson saying to me once, "We've just made a record for the England World Cup Squad with some blokes called New Order."

"You'll have a number one there, Robbo," I predicted. "No problem."

"Never, no way!" He was adamant. "There's no way that rubbish is going to get to number one!" So much for Captain Marvel's verdict on the supremely successful (and very good) "World in Motion".

Our progress into the semis meant that the second leg against our opponents, Borussia Dortmund, would clash with our Premier League match against Newcastle. Unless the season could be extended, we would be faced with four games in the last nine days of the season. This would also be our preparation for the European Champions' League final in Munich, if we beat the Germans. The Gaffer and the chairman were pushing hard for the extra week, but the players had no illusions that it would happen and were preparing for things to remain as they were. We played two Premier League games against Everton and Derby, with mixed results, before we flew out to Germany. A crucial match against Blackburn awaited us three days after that. So much could be lost in the space of seven days.

Our away leg against Dortmund was incredibly disappointing, as we just didn't play as we know we can. We travelled there early on the Monday and stayed an extra day so that our preparation could be as professional as possible for the Champions' League and Premier League games. The weather was very pleasant and we had a small, charming hotel which was very comfortable. On the Tuesday night we were on the bus ready to go to training – you always try to go to training at the same time as the game the following night. We were all waiting to start when the driver turned the key in the ignition and the complete lock barrel turned round. While the driver tried to get another bus, Albert the kit man strode forward clutching his bull-grips, looking as if he meant business. I thought he was ready to extract revenge for the delay, but he twisted things around under the bonnet and hot-wired the coach. I knew he used to work in Manchester Garages, but I thought he was a panel beater. It turns out he is a trained mechanic, and he put his skill to good use. We had already shouted down to those two Manc lads Nicky Butt and Paul Scholes to ask if there was any chance of either of them getting the bus started for us. They were a bit miffed at the suggestion, but Albert did the trick for us. He couldn't get the doors to shut, though, so we had to drive for a few miles with a representative of the travel company wedged in the space.

The stadium was superb but you couldn't say that about the pitch, which was in terrible condition. It was bumpy with great bare patches, especially in the middle, and it looked as though it would interfere with the quality of football. When we came back from training I picked up one of the many magazines the team had bought to while away the time. In *Total Sport*, in the middle of a thirty-odd page feature about the Red Devils, I came across an interview with Roy Keane who was doing his best to build up the McClair Training Myth to epic proportions. "Who is the worst trainer at the club?" asked the interviewer. I had a premonition about what his answer might be. "Brian McClair. He's the worst trainer in the world. He's only had one good day in training since he's been here." I immediately felt the burden of the international status my Irish colleague had bestowed on me. I did the only thing I could. I went to him and asked him if he could tell me the date of the one good day when I excelled myself, as I couldn't for the life of me remember when it was, so that I could commemorate its anniversary with a modest ceremony. He stared at me as if I'd grown another head.

For the game itself on Wednesday 9 April, the stadium was packed and the atmosphere was again magnificent. But though we created the better chances in the game, we just didn't play well. That's the sort of thing that has happened to us time and time again in Europe. Dortmund were very organized, but they achieved their win courtesy of a deflected goal. Peter Schmeichel and David May were both out of the team in unfortunate circumstances: Peter had a sore back and Maysie had picked up a freak injury in training on the Tuesday. Our plans were disrupted at a late stage, but that is not to say that the replacements didn't play their part. Raimond Van Der Gouw in particular made an excellent contribution in goal. Some commentators tried to suggest afterwards that Peter may have stopped the deflection, but I don't agree at all. There may have been other occasions in the match when Peter may not have dealt with balls as well as Raimond did. Still, we did keep the scoreline at 0–0 for seventy minutes. The German team were absolutely ecstatic. 1–0 is a great win at home, because no away goal has been conceded. I wouldn't say that they were anything to be feared, but they were an effective team with a mental toughness that made them hard to beat. They stopped us playing our game in this match and stuck to their own plan. At the risk of falling into national stereotypes, like all German teams they were very disciplined. We had to hope that we wouldn't regret the number of chances we had failed to take advantage of in this game.

Two controversial statements stirred things up at this time. The suggestion was made in the financial pages that it would cost United money to get into the Champions' League final. This remark was linked to bonus payments, and did not take into account the merchandising implications of a Championship win. Peter Schmeichel seems to have developed rather a knack for the contentious pronouncement this season. He was, however, absolutely astounded by the furore which followed his latest theory, namely that our current team would have beaten the 1968 European Cup-winning side 10–0. Afterwards he discussed his reasons with Kiddo and myself, arguing that players today were obviously more highly trained and more athletic. In terms of fitness alone, he believed that there was no way that the Champions of yore could hope to compete, as the pace would be far too fast for them.

"And of course you added the punchline, Peter," I asked him when he'd finished pontificating.

"What is that?" came the reply.

"The punchline – you know, 'But you've got to remember that the main reason we'd beat them is that they're all over fifty now!'"

"No." Peter was obviously not having any of it. "No, I do not wish to make a joke. I am completely serious about the matter and have been giving it much thought. I think it is clear that we would beat them at least by 10–0 for the reasons I have so carefully outlined. And I can't see why there would be any objections to that theory."

Kiddo and I gave each other an old fashioned look. We reckoned that there could be a few repercussions the day afterwards. It was bad enough him saying the current team would win, but 10–0 is a rather large margin.

Next day, Peter shook his head with total disbelief as he read the headlines in the English papers. "They have made a big story out of this? They have nothing else they can report? This is really making something out of nothing." He was soon to find out, when we returned to England, that it wasn't just the press who had decided to take his comments amiss, even though he meant no disrespect and was merely attempting to make a point about the changing nature of football. Paddy Crerand, United's midfield tiger of the 1968 team, was really very angry for one. A very deep apology followed. An understanding of history is needed if you are part of this club.

It does make you long for the days when the only questions put to footballers were those that required the answers "lager", "Ferrari", "steak and chips", "Marbella", "blue" and "George Benson". Now that we are moral arbiters, role models for youth, teenage heart-throbs, servants of the community and fashion leaders (I exclude myself from all those categories, of course), every word is fraught with danger. We'll probably have to go back to the former approach. If you never say anything more cerebral than "Over the moon" or "Whichever team scores more goals than the other one will win", there's no danger of putting your foot in it. Indeed, what else should footballers be talking about?

The anomalies of this year's fixture programme surfaced again: we had a free week following our game at Blackburn, for international reasons. It would have made sense to play our game against Newcastle then. We also had a "Championship decider" against Liverpool scheduled only four days before our make-or-break return match against Dortmund. In the end, the club was reduced to staging my testimonial game against

Celtic during the free week. Following our trip to Anfield on Saturday 23 April, we trained on the Sunday as part of the preparation which, with luck, would see us through to the final.

At this juncture, it was impossible not to daydream about European glory coming to the club once again. I have, of course, had success in Europe before; in my collection is a European Cup Winners' Cup medal from 1991 and a European Super Cup medal for 1992. The 1990/91 campaign was in many ways the exact opposite of the one we were engaged on this season. It began with very limited expectations. We drew the Hungarian team Pécsi Munkas in the first round, and we knew absolutely nothing about them. They came first to Old Trafford, where we put together an excellent performance to beat them 2–0. However, the manager warned us of the curious tendency exhibited by Eastern European teams. When you play them at their home grounds, they are a completely different team from when they played you away. Many Western European sides have been hammered, or (like United against Torpedo Moscow in 1991) gone out on penalties to teams that seemed to have had no form at all. We were therefore quite nervous of what lay in wait for us in Hungary.

Pécsi Munkas come from a very small town, and their stadium was one of the worst I have ever played at. The journey had been difficult, the night of the match was close and hot and the grass on the pitch was very long. It was almost claustrophobic playing in the tight ground. Our approach was cautious and measured, in line with the Gaffer's instructions, but we needn't have been so careful: they weren't very good. We won 1–0 (and 3–0 overall) thanks to my goal. I had the pleasure of scoring in every round except the final of that year's European competition. Aside from putting the ball in the net, my other vivid memory of the night was that there were people dressed as Father Christmas in the crowd. At the time, I thought it was because St. Nicholas was the patron saint of the area, but I've been told the Santas were English fans and it was a subterfuge to avoid the cameras beaming pictures of those "off on the sick" into the homes of their bosses. It certainly gave everything a very surreal air. All we needed were a few Easter bunnies to bounce up and down with them.

So on we progressed, still expecting to go out of the competition at any time. The draw favoured us once again when, in the next round, we drew Wrexham. We thought we might win this one, but in the first home leg they gave us a couple of early scares. Chris Armstrong, who later went to Tottenham, had two good chances to to score at the start. His finishing has improved since then. We eventually ended up 3–0 winners; I scored the third goal and it was quite a comfortable victory. For the return leg, even though Wrexham is only forty minutes down the road from Manchester, we had to go and stay in North Wales. According to the regulations, you have to be in the country where you are playing for twenty-four hours before the game. Our residential obligations satisfied, we won 2–0 and continued on our merry way.

We anticipated bigger problems with the French side Montpellier, our next opponents. Things would be very different against a team of their quality, who had in previous rounds disposed of PSV Eindhoven and Steaua Bucharest. We began by taking an early lead when I thumped home a shot from Lee Sharpe's cross, but then lost a goal and, to our disappointment, ended up with a 1–1 draw. But the second leg of the quarter finals was vastly different, once Clayton Blackmore had scored with a good strike from thirty yards out which rolled under the keeper, we were the dominant team.

Suddenly things were getting serious: we were in the semi finals. If you had a choice between one of three teams, and two of them were Barcelona and Juventus, you might think yourself fortunate if the team you eventually found yourself up against was Legia Warsaw. They had kindly (and unexpectedly) disposed of Sampdoria, but were judged the weakest team left. That was fine by us. Their ground was huge – I think they have one of the biggest pitches in Europe – and the sell-out crowd seemed to be composed largely of soldiers and policemen. The so-called weakest team left in the competition took the lead early on. We were lucky to equalize straight away, courtesy of a magnificently shinned shot from myself which didn't even hit the back of the net. We were in control after that and one of my strongest memories is of Lee Sharpe turning their right back inside out. He was taken off at half-time as he couldn't cope with Sharpey tormenting him. We ended up 3–1 winners, and after a little scare at home we went through to the finals. It was as simple as that. Those who believed that United had been very stuffy in the draw rubbed their hands when it came to the other team in the final – the one we had not been lucky enough to avoid. Barcelona were an excellent team, full of stars, but we beat them on the night. Even the Rotterdam weather did its bit for us; we enjoyed playing in the rain more than they did. I had the duty of man-marking Koeman, which I was praised for afterwards. Clayton cleared the ball off the line with a few minutes to go, but we held on. We stayed in Rotterdam the day afterwards and had a terrific celebration, though it was spoiled for me a lot as Maureen wasn't there to share it with me. She had given birth to Liam a week before.

In 1996/97, perhaps history would repeat itself and the unfancied underdogs would overcome the favourites in the final. Unfortunately, though my daydream came true in essence, I got the fine detail wrong.

I must have been asked about our return match against Borussia twenty times beforehand and my answer was always the same: it would be the hardest game of our season. There was a palpable air of confidence about the Germans. When they took to the pitch, they seemed to believe that whatever happened they could score a goal. If they did, we would be left with the very difficult task of scoring three to win.

Ryan Giggs took my place on the bench. As UEFA rules always appear to be enforced more strictly in England than anywhere else I was once again banned from my accustomed viewing position near the halfway line. Perhaps I was deemed to be endangering public safety from there. I had taken precautions to ensure that I had a good seat for the match, keeping back one of the tickets I had obtained for friends so that I could sit next to Maureen and, with luck, watch our progress into the final in her company. We had a brilliant start with a disallowed goal.

Everyone around me was out of their seats, but I didn't bother getting up as I had seen the infringement by David May. "It's a foul," I said, flatly. We had put them under pressure right from the beginning. After eight minutes, though, there was a major departure from the script when Dortmund took the lead through Ricken. I was stunned. For a time it seemed as if I was watching the game in slow motion; I couldn't really believe that the ball had ended up in our goal. The Dortmund player, in what seemed like a vast expanse of time, turned and shot; Peter went down and I thought, "That's never gone in, has it?" But it had. It was very cruel that the goal should again be partly the result of a deflection, but we did have another eighty-two minutes to do something about it. Our play up to that point suggested that we were capable of scoring three goals. Well, that's the thought that was keeping me going, anyway.

Of greater concern as the match went on was the number of gilt-edged chances all of our forward players were failing to convert. I was big on rhetorical questions during this match. "Surely we're going to put one of these away sooner or later?" I thought, but by the time we did (only for it to be disallowed once more) it was too late, anyway. The match statistics afterwards told the story. We had twenty shots, and though these can sometimes give a distorted picture, this time they were spot on. I've never seen a team defend like Dortmund for so long and be fortunate enough to keep us out for the whole match. It just wasn't to be.

There were tears on the pitch at the close while the enormous disappointment sank in. Everybody at the club, right down to the non-playing staff, took it very hard. One of the restaurant stewards, Bill, had to take the champagne to the Dortmund dressing room for their post-victory celebrations, and he found it very, very difficult. The Gaffer came into the dressing room at full-time and told the players they had proved they were good enough to win the Champions' League. Those were no empty words intended merely to console. It was especially gratifying that the Dortmund team and fans spoke so highly of the sportsmanship of the United fans in defeat, even though it must have stuck in our fans' teeth. Certainly, in a small outpost of Caledonia in Wilmslow, one lone Scot was taking it all very badly.

Over the next few days, the younger players managed to lift themselves much more easily than the older ones who had grown to believe that the trophy was within reach. The elasticity of youth allows them to believe they will be back there again next season, but at the risk of sounding like the voice of doom, there are no such guarantees in football. We may never progress as far in the Champions' League again, and the changes to the structure of the competition probably lengthen the odds. With six groups of four qualifiers, United may very well find themselves in a group with Juventus, Barcelona and Glasgow Rangers.

My parting words on the night, as I began the descent into a very, very bad mood that was to stay with me for days, was that Dortmund seemed to have the luck with them. Though Juventus were obviously the better side, the Germans could easily win the competition – not that I put any money on that. It transpired that I should have risked a few bob. Dortmund, like United in Rotterdam in 1991, having been told for a few weeks that there was little point in even turning up, overturned the form book on the night and won the prize. Even though I had had the pleasure of collecting my fourth Premier League medal by the time the Champions' League final came around, I was again despondent, because that could so easily have been us.

You can always overturn the form books on the night, though it doesn't happen often. Some things are just too fantastic. After one match this season, a bloke thrust a crumpled piece of paper at me and demanded, "Choccy, can you write on this, 'IOU £1.09'? I've just had a bet on you to score the first goal." The odds were apparently 200–1. But it was an equally unlikely event which saw United achieve their second European success since 1968. On 19 November 1991, shortly after our elimination from the Cup Winners' Cup in the second round, after failing to recover from two appalling lapses of concentration away against Atletico Madrid we met Red Star Belgrade in the European Super Cup at Old Trafford. It was just the start of the troubles in

Yugoslavia and it wasn't possible to play a leg over there. Red Star were anxious to play the game, and suggested a compromise: a one-off match at Old Trafford. We were comprehensively hammered by a terrific Red Star team and we crowned it all by winning 1–0. If ever a victory was undeserved, this was it. The honour of scoring the winning goal fell to me in the sixty-seventh minute. If I'd been playing for them, I would have been absolutely gutted. Savicevic was unbelievable; his touch and running were a joy to watch, until he went off at half-time with a pulled hamstring and we all cheered with relief. Soon after this game, he signed for Milan. Panchev, who also moved on to Inter Milan and had forty-odd goals to his credit that season, could not score for the life of him. It began to look as if he was deliberately trying to miss. He headed over the bar from six yards out and seemed bound to score umpteen other times. I have a very impressive medal from that evening. Later in life, when everyone has forgotten what that competition actually was, I will embellish its significance.

What a great shame we won't be competing for the World Club Championship next year. The Man of the Match wins a car as it is sponsored by Honda. Apparently, the South American player who usually wins sells his prize and shares out the proceeds with his team mates. I can't imagine one of our players doing that voluntarily.

So, instead of being measured for our European Champions' League suits, we had "only the Premier League" left to stop our season becoming meaningless. No Cup success means you never heard the Joe Strummer song which would have given a new respectability to the United repertoire. Once we had been eliminated from the European Cup, I received a letter which stated, "This project has now been shelved", which somehow seems a fitting epitaph on both.

11

Leagues apart

"Would you rather Labour won the election or Manchester United the League?"

We kept our place as leaders in the Premier League throughout our European adventures.

The League match before the Porto quarter final was against Coventry. It gets my vote as the most bizarre of the season; though it took place on 1 March, 1 April would have been much more appropriate. Coventry actually scored three goals in this game but, paradoxically, lost 3–1. It all seemed normal enough when we kicked off, but it wasn't long before strange events began to occur. After four minutes, Gary Breen, the young player in the left back position for Coventry, decided to open the scoring. Eric Cantona took possession of the ball and knocked it through to Andy Cole. Andy duly gave chase, but the pass was overhit and it was evident that Breen was always going to get there first. He probably wished he had been a bit slower to react when he promptly swept the ball with great aplomb past the goalkeeper, into the corner of his own net. From the bench, the whole scene was amazing to watch. Breen's misfortune certainly did much to settle United's nerves, while doing very little for his own – or those of Gordon Strachan, the Coventry manager.

Only a minute later, Andy Cole did his best to clear a dangerous ball for Coventry, but Eoin Jess was on hand to spare our striker's blushes by deflecting the ball some distance into the empty Coventry goal – though

Andy still got the credit on the scoresheet. "If Coventry score another for us," I reflected idly, "It will all be over." Although we were concentrating very hard during this game, the benefits of a relatively easy win pre-Porto were obvious. After gratefully receiving the gift of a two-goal lead, we decided it would be a good idea if we scored a few ourselves, but curiously found it far more difficult to find the Coventry net than the Sky Blues had done. The number of chances we failed to convert before the half-time whistle blew was almost comic. Our luck seemed to change when, two minutes into the second half, Andy Cole played a through pass for Karel Poborsky to use his pace to spring the offside trap and thump in a low, hard shot. Finally we scored in our own right. The manager then decided he could afford to change it around to bring people off for a rest. Phil Neville (back for his first senior game after recovering from glandular fever) and I came on – just as all the defending had to be done. Before Andy scored, Coventry's men had looked really demoralized, but when you are 3–0 down you have nothing to lose. They began to push forward to good effect and could have scored three or four goals – on their own behalf, I mean. Peter was forced into some important saves and the defence also put in one or two good blocks to preserve our advantage. Eventually, near the end, Coventry deservedly pulled one back with a fine goal from Huckerby, their best player on the afternoon, who looked very lively against us both times this season. Our victory opened a gap of four points between ourselves and Liverpool.

After speeding down the fast lane of the motorway on Wednesday 5 March, on the Saturday we were back trundling down our own personal B road against Sunderland. I can't put into words how I felt after the game. The Gaffer decided that he had to rest some of the team who had performed so magnificently because of the considerable effort that they had all expended. Against the Portuguese, Pally had given one of his best performances of the season, but had struggled through the second half with a groin injury that had to be given time to heal. Ryan was feeling his hamstring. Cole and Solskjaer needed a break after running themselves ragged. For those of us who replaced them, Jordi Cruyff, Karel Poborsky and myself among them, it was a very bad day. We couldn't get anything right; there was no rhythm at all to our play. Sunderland were a team fighting for their lives and they played that way. They deserved everything they got out of this match. We gave away two poor goals from defensive errors and our own contribution to the score sheet was provided by the other side when a free kick by Beckham was inexplicably helped into the net. The kindest opinion ventured about my own performance was "useless", and I think that was fair comment. I was so disappointed.

Still, we comforted ourselves – or tried to comfort ourselves – with the thought that there is always one game like this every year in the Championship run-up. The 0–1 defeat by Oldham in March 1993 springs to mind, or the match we lost to Wimbledon by a single goal at Selhurst Park in 1994. This kind of match is always portrayed by the media as a "struggling" or "lesser" team knocking the complacency out of a bunch of arrogant superstars, while they fight for their survival with praiseworthy grit. I can assure you that this was not the case against Sunderland. The changes to the team were made on the basis of careful calculation about the injuries and tiredness of the usual first-team players, even if it didn't work out.

Once again, fixture congestion became an issue and, once again, United were accused of arrogance and self-interest. The Gaffer's broadsides against the envy and hatred many clubs feel towards United's success were dismissed as paranoia. You can't claim that such jealousy doesn't exist; it is only natural. After all, we keep shoving ourselves into peoples' faces by going on winning and attracting huge attention. As for our Gaffer being paranoid, I recall a time he had the dressing rooms swept for bugs as "confidential" information was leaking out. Conspiracy theories have their place, but as I saw it, the source of the leak had to be either a player or a staff member. I could have told him to save his money. Players can't keep anything to themselves: you don't need to spend a fortune on sophisticated electronic listening devices to tap into the secret conversations in any football club; it's much cheaper and faster to buy a player a pint. As far as the ongoing campaign to secure an extension to the season was concerned, I would also have advised the club not to waste its time, though I suppose it was worth a try. Did anyone seriously believe that, if asked, either Arsenal, Newcastle, Liverpool or any other club in the Premier League would agree to something which would give Manchester United any advantage whatsoever? "Hello, is that Jack Walker/Sir John Hall? Would you agree to adding an extra week on to the season to give Manchester United a better chance of winning the Premier League, because they might not win it if they have to play four games in nine days?" I think not.

It may never happen to Manchester United again, but if a team is very successful in both home and domestic competitions, there will always be fixture problems for as long as there are so many clubs in the Premier League. You can't have a rearrangement of the programme, so you'll just have to reduce the number of matches. Though other clubs may pay lip service to the pious thought that it would be good if British clubs did well in Europe next year, it's no use to them if they're watching this success from the First Division. The decision to reduce the Premier League still further has to be taken out of the hands of people who won't, or more accurately, can't afford to make it.

I've never had an enjoyable day (or night) at Goodison Park; the matches there are always really hard going for United. We faced Everton only three days after the Porto draw and contributed to a really dreadful game. By the end, we were holding on for a win. We didn't play particularly well, and the way they played, launching the ball forward to Duncan Ferguson and feeding off the scraps, didn't make it all that attractive a proposition for the fans. Our first goal came from nothing really. Solskjaer hit the ball forward and it went in, though that may have had something to do with goalkeepers being a bit off form on Merseyside this year. There may have been a bobble, but it did look to us as if

Paul Gerrard, the Everton goalkeeper, should have had it. So by half-time we were 1–0 in the lead from the only shot on goal we had had in the whole of the first forty-five minutes. For an Everton tie things were going quite well, though Gary Pallister picked up an injury and had to come off just before the half-time whistle. In the second half we had no real problems, and stretched our lead when we were gifted a goal after their goalie missed a cross completely. The ball hit Eric on the nose, dropped on to his foot and bounced in. He denied it was an accident, claiming that he planned to do it.

Duncan Ferguson is a very good player and against United he always looks exceptionally dangerous. He was supposed to have elbowed David May in the throat, but I don't think Duncan meant it. If he had, Maysie probably wouldn't have got up off the pitch. I was very disappointed that the brush with an Evertonian elbow didn't stop Maysie talking. It's not that I wished him any serious injury, of course; I was just hoping for a lightly crushed windpipe. David does talk all the time without actually ever saying anything. It's a continuous stream of nonsense, some of which, I suppose, can occasionally be entertaining. Actually, I think he has become my apprentice and will take over when I leave. He's professed himself a great admirer of my wit, without really having any choice in the matter.

In addition to making waves by pursuing an extension to the season, United also were hammered for what was perceived to be the manager's selfish stance in the club versus country debate. People also exaggerated what the manager did or didn't say; as I remember it, all he said was that he could appreciate why you would want a strong national team and it is important to qualify for the World Cup. However, there will be players (largely from Manchester United) who have played sixty games for their club in a season before being selected – and don't forget that all those games are very competitive. But it can't be just a one-way process; surely it is just as important for the players to be fresh for the start of the new season? It might not take long for them to recover physically, but mentally you need a break, no matter how old you are. All players want to represent their country; it is an honour for them. If I wanted to play for Scotland in the past I would have gone regardless – and I don't think the Gaffer would have stopped me. He has not prevented anyone who wasn't injured from going to represent their country – in any games.

Just when we had the opportunity to pull away at the top of the League, we turned in another dismal performance, this time at home against Derby on 5 April. Our defending touched new lows: if we had defended like that against any team we would have had problems. We had a chance to score at the start, but then things went from pretty bad to much, much worse and Derby scored two goals. One came from Paolo Wanchope, who picked up the ball at outside right and ran all that way through to score. We watched him cut right through the middle, as if to say, "Look at that! He's going through us like a knife through butter!" We were lucky not to concede at least another one. After the break, we scored right away to put us in with the chance of a point. Eric took his chance beautifully, but then Peter Schmeichel and Gary Pallister decided to add to the comedy of the occasion by misunderstanding each others' intentions. Sometimes half-time can't come soon enough in a match like this. We took the opportunity to reorganize, and then did something really stupid. Neither Peter nor Pally would accept responsibility. No matter how good you are you can still make mistakes. Ronny Johnsen slipped and the ball came off the post after the other pair had messed it up. Dean Sturridge scored Derby's third goal as a result of this catalogue of errors. He should have really shown us up by getting down on his hands and knees and heading the ball into the net, laughing hysterically all the while. Solskjaer gave us some hope with a fine goal which he controlled well on his chest, but defensively we were all over the place – for the whole of the match.

The headlines afterwards saw the result as a great moral triumph for the intrinsically worthy Derby against the undeserving, complacent United. "United's overpaid superstars seriously miscalculated as they arrogantly blah, blah, blah..." You know the form. But complacency wasn't our problem; playing very badly was. We didn't believe it was going to be a stroll but we just couldn't find our rhythm, and Derby County had a much better day than we did.

We lost again to Dortmund the following Wednesday, our second defeat in five days. (The last time we had two consecutive defeats in all competitions was at the end of October and the beginning of November 1996.) Next, the fixture computer had obliged us with a tie at friendly Ewood Park on 12 April. We had made it that much more difficult for ourselves after our previous Saturday's dismal showing. The first patch of decent football we managed to play, where we passed the ball a few times to our own players rather than Blackburn's, resulted in a goal. Andy Cole held off two men after a through ball from Cantona and slotted the ball to the right of Flowers. Then we conceded an equalizer by not reacting quickly enough to the ball being cleared, exactly the same way we had given away one to Blackburn Rovers in 1995/96. Raimond, deputizing for Peter whose back was still painful, might have been unsighted but his defence let him down. The score remained level until our second patch of excellent play, which culminated in a great shot from Paul Scholes made possible by a super pass from Andy on the edge of the area.

You don't ever expect to see it, but when Eric misses two penalties in the same season it is something to tell your grandchildren. This time, Flowers dived the right way to save his shot. We were very slow in reacting when the ball came out off the keeper, because the whole team believed it was as good as in the back of the net when Eric stepped up to put it on the spot. It didn't look as though his miss would have any bearing on the outcome of the game; we increased our lead after a terrific bit of skill from Andy, who was having one of his best matches in a United shirt. He dribbled the ball with fantastic control around two defenders before cutting it back to Eric in the penalty area. Eric duly scored from ten yards out.

Although we were heading towards victory at 3–1, we began to feel a bit uncomfortable that we were making things that easy for ourselves. So we gave away a soft, silly goal to keep us on edge and make ourselves have to defend with an air of urgency for the last three minutes. We had every encouragement from our fans, who were magnificent. All the singers had congregated in one place and kept up a constant barrage of songs and noise.

After the game, three urchins decided to climb on to our coach, and the amount of time they managed to spend on there demonstrated how difficult it is sometimes to deal with the public without encouraging lawsuits. The small boys, who were messing around at the front, all fitted the description "character". We told them to shift a few times, but they just ignored us and carried on fiddling around. When one of them finally climbed into the driver's seat, as the official "responsible person" I decided that I needed to take some action. I could see him knocking the brake off and the coach rolling forward and killing someone. I switched the engine off, assumed what I hoped was an air of authority and asked them politely to remove themselves. They looked at me in precisely the same way my own children do and stayed put, unabashed. I was forced to raise my voice in a footballer's shout, and after a bit of deliberation that seemed to convince them it might be better if they left. You have to be very careful in these situations.

The fixtures had been staggered over the weekend for television purposes, which seemed to give us an advantage. We had won our game on the Saturday; our nearest opponents all failed to win their matches that weekend. We knew by experience that, despite the fact that we had only five Premiership matches left, there was still a strong possibility that we might not take the title.

United has had two last-minute, nailbiting climaxes to the Championship during my time at club. We lost one, we won the other. But my most dramatic, close-run finish was at Celtic in the 1985/86 season. For its final match, Celtic had to go to Paisley and defeat St Mirren by three goals. Our rivals, Hearts, who had been running away with the League all that season, only needed a draw at Dundee for the trophy to be theirs. It was, as I remember it, a beautiful sunny day, fitting weather for a match played at Love Street. I was struck by the over-whelming belief that we were going to win the Championship, even though the odds had to be in favour of the Edinburgh club. It was a dream match in many respects. We played some superb football and, by half-time, were winning by the virtually unassailable margin of 4–0. But our success would be immaterial if Hearts maintained their 0–0 half-time score.

Five minutes from time, the St Mirren keeper came forward to collect the ball and suddenly the Celtic fans behind him erupted. It didn't take much for those of us out on the pitch to work out what had just happened at Dens Park. The photographers on the touchline thought we might need some clarification. They shouted to us, "They've scored, Dundee have taken the lead against Hearts! Albert Craig has scored!" "Yes!" I bellowed with great originality, and I punched the air before going out on to the right wing. When I got there, the linesman whispered to me, "Choccy, they've scored. We've won it!" I looked at him in disbelief. The ground was full of Celtic fans that day: most of the 17,000 spectators, and one of the officials. We still had our own game to play to the finish, but by this time we were 5–0 up and our concentration had understandably wavered. The Celtic players were all talking to each other as they passed the ball around, asking how much longer Hearts had to go before the whistle. Their match had kicked off two minutes after ours. Hearts ended up losing 2–0. Our victory came after a United-style second half of the season, in which we put together a run of sixteen League games without defeat. Though delirious with joy at my first Championship victory, I did feel a moment's sadness for my friend, John Colquhoun of Hearts, who saw their season fall apart in the space of one week. But it was only a moment.

This year, the same John Còlquhoun had the honour of being voted Rector of Edinburgh University and I was talking to him about it on the telephone.

"Listen," he said, "I've tried to get this changed, but they won't budge on it. I'm going to be carried around in a sedan chair at the ceremony."

"Great!" I told him, "When is it? This is something I have just got to see!"

"No way! You're not coming. It will be bad enough without you being there!"

He wouldn't have been able to stop me going along to enjoy his discomfort if I hadn't been off in Europe at the time.

In 1996/97, for the second season running, I was in line for two League medals. The Reserves were edging ever closer to their annual win in the Pontin's League when they took on Everton at Goodison. However, though we usually win this competition, we seemed to have caught the first team disease of dragging things out teasingly for as long as possible. The most memorable event in this match, apart from the five goals, was the half-time entertainment. A dog gave a demonstration of goalkeeping; I couldn't seem to get away from performing canines this season. We won't be signing him as a replacement for Raimond van der Gouw as it was far more trouble clearing up after the dog than the Dutchman.

The Reserves took a 3–1 lead and were cruising along comfortably until Raimond threw the ball out to Paul Scholes near the halfway line. It was intercepted by the Everton centre half, who blooted it right back up the pitch over Raimond's head. I still don't know why Raimond didn't run back to try to stop it; he might have got the ball. Maybe the dog would have done better with it. For the last three minutes we were reduced to defending like crazy. I endeared myself to the referee by continually asking him, "How long have we got? We can't have much more to go, surely?" When he got down finally to thirty seconds, I stood next to him chanting, "One Mississippi, two Mississippis, three Mississippis..." He blew the whistle when I reached twenty-seven Mississippis. Perhaps I should ask Maureen to buy me a stopwatch.

I was booked in the game, not for the serious offence of irritating the life out of the officials, but for kicking the ball away. The irony was that I wasn't actually doing that at all. I was, in fact, trying to kick it at one of my teammates who was annoying me. It came on to my left foot and my kick was so accurate that it missed and went sixty yards into the stand. Why I was so furious I can't remember – perhaps it was because he had given the ball away, or something like that – but it was probably more just bad temper. I was Mr Angry all game, stomping around and muttering under my breath. But my bark was worse than my bite.

Our next game in our circuitous pursuit of Pontin's League glory was also close to home. Jim Ryan, the Reserve team coach, offered me a lift up to Bolton and his son accompanied us in the back of the car. Jim was driving on autopilot, though neither of his two passengers realized it, guided by a powerful homing instinct. We were halfway along the road to Scotland before Jim came round and noticed he was going the wrong way. We turned back quickly, without really having any idea of where we were. Eventually we just found the ground out of complete luck, as in the "we'll try a left here" school of navigation. Anyway, we got there in sufficient time. I've only ever been late once. It was for a Reserve game, at home. I'd been pottering around making my leisurely way into work for a three o'clock kick-off, when it suddenly dawned on me that the kick-off had been brought forward an hour. I looked at my watch – quarter to two. Unbelievably, I was about to be too late to play in a match which the kids and Maureen were coming to watch. Sweating profusely, I made it in time to persuade them to let me turn out as I would never have been allowed to forget it.

Our current Bolton fixture had been changed; it was supposed to have been the last ever match at Burnden Park, but it wouldn't have done for the farewells to the ground to be said at a Reserve tie. As soon as we entered the away dressing room, a mood of deep depression fell upon our squad. It was uncanny the way we all began to feel disorientated and our spirits sagged. If I was the designer of Bolton's new showcase stadium, I would acknowledge that some things about the old ground were just too valuable to lose and recreate the whole of the away team dressing room, unaltered, in their new home. As light neither penetrates nor escapes this godforsaken place, it's a perfect spot for an interrogation. After five minutes trapped in there, you would tell anybody everything and anything they wanted to know just to get out. As I sat down staring at the plain blue gloss-painted walls, I wondered if I could be bothered tieing up my socks because suddenly it all seemed so pointless. Then, while slumped in melancholy reverie, I worked out what was happening to me. It's no wonder they've had so many great results at home: once the away team has been in their dressing-room for the whole hour preceding the game, their spirit would have been broken. We have ways of making you lose. Next year, if Bolton start dropping points at home, it won't be because of the stiffer competition they face in the Premier League, it will be because they no longer have the prison-style decor of their old away dressing rooms.

We did rally ourselves to make it out on to the pitch for kick off. Another bumper Reserve gate had come to watch us: 6,000 people, attracted by the sincere love and admiration that fans of Bolton feel for Manchester United. Some choice and pleasant songs were sung in our honour, and we responded to the tributes by scoring the first goal, courtesy of Ben Thornley. His dream start was soon soured. He was sent off after becoming entangled with one of the young Bolton players, though to my mind he was a bit unlucky to be shown the red card. After the sending-off, it turned into one of the worst games you have ever seen in your whole life. Bolton attacked for the whole of the second half while we defended with increasing desperation. For Wanderers' fans, longing for a victory over the swollen-headed glamour boys of United Reserves, the frustration at the failure of their team to find an equalizer became unbearable. At one point I became a particular target for abuse. No prizes for guessing the song which became my theme for the rest of the game. The match steadily deteriorated until the final whistle, when it improved beyond all recognition – because we won. I smiled sweetly at the Bolton crowd as we went in and gave them a cheery wave. I wonder if looking nauseatingly pleased with yourself can be deemed behaviour likely to incite crowd trouble? It certainly stirred them up. I went off to shower and change if I could be bothered once I'd stepped back into the dressing room.

By contrast, the Reserves' next outing against Oldham at Old

Trafford on Thursday 2 April saw us dominate the game yet barely scrape a 1–1 draw. We had three very good chances in the first half and it was difficult to see how the ball didn't make it into the Oldham net for the first two. However, with their only chance of the first half Oldham broke away and took the lead. In the second half Andy Cole scored a fine individual goal with a low, blistering shot which beat the keeper. He was pulled off with twenty minutes to go and replaced by Simon Davies. Despite constant pressure for what remained of the game we failed to score again to win.

The match at Oldham gave a glimpse of what going to see a football match used to be like. While the game was going on, gangs of teenagers paraded about with their friends; little kids ran up and down the steps every few minutes and leant against the metal barrier around the pitch. And one thing you haven't seen at Old Trafford for a very, very long time: when the teams changed ends, the crowd got up and went to sit at the other end of the only stand which was open to watch the goal United was attacking. Tickets for the Reserves are very cheap, and the five thousand or so who come will recognize a lot of the players: Paul Scholes, Andy Cole, Jordi Cruyff, Raimond van der Gouw and myself have appeared regularly in the first team (and, by the end of the season, two of these would be in the England international squad); Terry Cooke, Michael Clegg, Chris Casper, Ben Thornley and John O'Kane have also turned out in League and Cup games. Tonight we were shuffling rather than marching towards glory.

The following Monday the Reserves were to play Liverpool at Gigg Lane, but for once I wouldn't be turning out for them. The day afterwards was the date fixed for my testimonial match, and I hoped that Kiddo and the Gaffer would at least name me in the squad for it. The reading public was treated to a variety of features about me which formed part of the general publicity. They largely followed the line of, "He reads the broadsheets not the tabloids and began a degree so therefore, in footballing terms, he must be an intellectual. He has had to be content with sitting on the bench and has accepted it uncomplainingly."

There is a grain of truth somewhere in all that. But they would insist on saying I was thirty four; that extra year they added is very important to a footballer. Football years are rather like dog years in this respect.

The exception to the "Brian McClair, loyal but dull (and thirty-four)" tributes was a feature in *90 Minutes*, leading with my observation that I always believed my body would deteriorate before my brain (though they both seem to be going off at the same rate). The person they sent to interview me was so young I could hardly believe it. I'm used to my teammates looking like children, but now it's happening to reporters and everyone else. I was very nice to him in deference to his tender years, even when he asked me, "Would you rather Labour won the election or Manchester United won the League?" I suppose this was meant to be the sort of intelligent question that a "thinker" like myself would relish getting my teeth into, rather than just plain stupid. Someone should have warned him that after nearly seventeen years in professional football, I have perfected the art of avoiding any type of serious reflection. I answered that particular gem by staring hard at him for several seconds. Well, what was I supposed to say? Yes, no, maybe? Then he followed that up by asking me what Pat Nevin and I got up to when we went to gigs together, probably in the hope that I would tell him that we were forever snorting cocaine in the toilets. Complaining about our sciatica and talking about our families would be nearer the mark. In the absence of any answer which he deemed sufficiently exciting, he had to liven things up by rambling on about stage diving and biting the heads off chickens. No comment.

12

Homage to Caledonia

"There's too many people, Dad!"

The coach doors opened with a hiss of air, and from inside came the unmistakeable strains of a song that I must have heard thousands of times. "And if you know your history, it's enough to make your heart go woah-oh-oh!" I knew exactly what they meant. The fluorescent yellow-and-black striped passengers spilled out on to the Old Trafford fore-court. It was my testimonial day, and it was starting off very well indeed. The Celtic supporters' coaches had already begun to arrive and the celebratory spirit was well in evidence. And it was still only midday; there were eight hours to go before kick-off. This particular group had come from Dundee, not just from Glasgow, which meant they travelled some three hundred miles to be there. We didn't only want Celtic for this this match because I had played for them for four years, but because, as everyone knows, their fans are the very best guests to invite to a party if you want a tremendous atmosphere. We knew that we were assured of a great night, whatever else happened. We had sold all 5,800 tickets in Glasgow, and on the night exiled Celtic supporters would come from all over to see their team play. Everything conspired to make this a perfect evening as the weather was unseasonably warm. It had been pleasant enough in the morning when I woke up, by lunchtime the sunshine was brilliant and shirt-sleeve hot.

There have been mutterings that Celtic fans are in too much demand for testimonials. As Paddy Crerand put it in my testimonial programme, "The Celts will come to support their team…They will be here in their thousands tonight, as they always are when the Bhoys visit Old Trafford, determined as ever to have a good time." Paddy pointed out that I was the fourth player to move from Celtic to United since the Second World War (the other players were Jimmy Delaney, Lou Macari and Paddy himself). For each of us, the move didn't go down well at the time, whatever people have come to think of it since then. And the Celts had come, in their thousands, and were there because they love to follow their team and know how to enjoy a day out south of the border.

I had four memorable years at Celtic, won one League Championship in an unforgettable fashion, a Scottish Cup in the hundredth Cup final in 1985, two League Cup Runners' Up medals and scored a fair amount of goals. The record books show that I was the leading goal scorer in all four seasons I was there, netting ninety-nine goals in 145 League appearances. In 1986/87 I won the Golden Boot and the Scottish Player of the Year and Scottish Football Writers' Player of the Year. I scored forty-one goals that season, but we didn't win anything. That Celtic side certainly was exciting to watch, but exasperated the supporters. We had no trouble conjuring up goals, but we didn't have the same success in keeping them out. Throughout this period the Celts' main rival for honours was not Rangers but Aberdeen. The challenge to the Old Firm monopoly in the early eighties was, of course, masterminded by that footballing genius, the Gaffer.

I came to sign for Celtic after I had been to Mexico with Scotland for the summer in the Fifa Under-20 World Cup squad. It was the first time I'd ever been abroad on a football trip, and for three weeks I lived, breathed and ate football all the time. It was excellent experience. The squad went first to Colorado Springs to acclimatize because of the high altitude in Mexico, and our preparations had gone well. In the tournament itself, we progressed through to the quarter finals and we played in the Azteca Stadium in front of 90,000 fans. We won the game 1–0, and the crowd threw everything from oranges to bricks at the Mexican players. Most of us were eighteen or nineteen years old and were stunned at having to dodge the missiles as we came off the pitch, none of which were actually aimed at us. Our next match was on the Saturday during the warmest part of the day. Our coach told us there was bound to be a huge crowd to see us after our previous performance, which was a nonsense as we weren't playing against the Mexicans this time. Only 10,000 people were rattling around in the enormous stadium.

I'd done quite well in the competition and on my return I was thinking about abandoning my degree course and becoming a full-time player. I knew there was a possibility that if Charlie Nicholas left Celtic to go to England they'd be looking out for someone to replace him. Nothing had been said to me formally; but (probably like a lot of strikers in Scotland) I lived in hope. One night I got a phone call from Jock Wallace, manager of Motherwell and a man who didn't waste his words.

"Aye, son, ah've sould ye."

"Eh?"

"Ah've sould ye – tae Celtic. Come 'n' see me."

So I went to Mum and Dad and said, "Jock Wallace sais he's sould me – tae Celtic."

They were naturally concerned as they wanted me to finish at university, but I knew right then there was no way I could sign for Celtic and continue my course. It had been hard enough while I was at Motherwell.

I went to Fir Park to sort things out, but I had already decided I wasn't going to put any obstacles in the way of my joining such a great club. Jock Wallace advised me to ask for a signing-on fee of £10,000, then took me in to see Billy McNeill. Motherwell were in financial difficulties at the time and were forced to accept the transfer price that Celtic offered for me – £90,000. The Motherwell commercial manager called this sum "derisory" in the testimonial programme. Modesty prevents me from adding any comment of my own.

I was summoned into the office where Billy McNeill was waiting. There I was, only nineteen, facing the ex-Celtic captain, a player of huge achievements. Later, after I left for England, he would lead Celtic to success in his second period of management there. He told me he wanted me to sign a four-year contract and we discussed what my wage would be.

"Ah'll give ye £5,000 fir a signing-on fee," he concluded.

"Bit ah want ten," I croaked

"Yir a greidy wee man. You'll have five and like it."

"Oh, OK."

And so I became a Celtic player.

My parents were still far from sure about it all, but for me, four years playing with Celtic for that sort of money was a dazzling prospect. I couldn't believe it had happened and that I hadn't really had the chance to discuss it with anyone. Indeed, it had come about without very much involvement on my part at all. One moment I was on Motherwell's books and the next I had signed for Celtic. The amount of press attention was amazing. Photographers began arriving at our house. I was Billy McNeill's last signing for Celtic, before he left to manage Aston Villa. It was not necessarily a purchase that everyone agreed with. One fan was quoted as saying that I would never score any goals for the club and my "derisory" transfer fee was considered a waste of money for an untried player. I "only" scored 120 in my four years as a Celt, mind.

Davie Hay, who had been my manager at Motherwell before Jock Wallace had intended to take up a job in Florida, but when this fell through he filled Billy McNeill's place at Celtic. It was a positive change for me – or so I felt; it was good to have someone I knew in charge. I turned out for the Reserves in my first game for the club and scored twice. This meant that I was promoted to the first team. The first full game I played for the Bhoys was at Dundee. We won 6–2 and this time I scored four goals. I felt I had already done enough to prove the doubters wrong and to stake a claim for my first-team place. Then we went to Denmark on the following Wednesday for the second leg of a European tie (we'd won the first leg 1–0 at Parkhead) – and I was dropped! Davie Hay reckons that I never understood his thinking on this. He's absolutely right, and I still don't. I did come off the bench during the match, though, and we won the tie comfortably.

Back to the present. The coach from Dundee was soon followed by others. Then the T-shirt and souvenir sellers set up their stalls and began to parade up and down with their hats, scarves and flags. They seemed to know something about the potential size of this evening's crowd. I toyed with the idea of asking them for a few quid as commission, but I didn't want to look grasping. I liked the idea that everybody might get something out of the evening. The Celtic fans continued to arrive throughout the afternoon, but didn't spend all their time drinking in the pubs or sitting around on the pavements. Thanks to the Metro tram, you can be in the centre of Manchester within five or so minutes, and a few thousand congregated there.

It was, however, only 15 April, not the traditional time for testimonial matches of this type. They are supposed to be the culmination of the tax-free year of money-raising that you are allowed. The reason it took place well before the end of the season was inextricably bound up with the controversy about the pile-up of fixtures. Arsène Wenger, the Arsenal manager (who had just returned from Japan, as our Gaffer had been keen to point out in a press conference), was swift to say that I should have held my testimonial game at the end of May, as one of his long-serving players was doing. By a curious coincidence, this player happened to be Nigel Winterburn. Everyone is entitled to their own opinion – no matter how wrong it may be.

We'd had a date at the end of the season, but because Celtic were involved in the European Champions' League preliminaries we had to change it. It became clear that it was impossible to fix a firm date, and we would have to leave it and leave it. Every time we came up with a possible slot, there was some obstacle or another. We sent a list of dates to Celtic and we thought we had sorted things out – 15 or 18 May were the most likely, avoiding the Scottish Cup final which they still hoped to contest, and meant a chance of sun. But the Celts had agreed to go to Dublin that week. By this juncture, it was obvious we would have to move the match forward rather than back. Sunday 13 April was a possibility for a while, until it became the semi-final day between Middlesbrough and Chesterfield. We thought we'd struggle to find any day at all, until Celtic suddenly said they could make 15 April. As soon as we had the date, any publicity was good publicity, whether people agreed with the timing of the match or not. In fact, no other match could be played in that week. In order for us to have played our League game against Newcastle then rather than in the last week of the season (when there would probably have to be three games, on the Bank Holiday Monday, the Thursday and the Sunday), the Magpies would have had to change the timing of their game with Chelsea. However, Coventry also would have to be involved, and they wouldn't agree to a rearrangement of their tie with Chelsea. Coventry's attitude was hardly surprising, as their only concern had to be avoiding relegation. There is nothing in the Premier League rules which can force a team to change the date of their fixtures. My testimonial committee gladly grabbed the opportunity of 15 April when it was offered them.

This left us with fourteen days to prepare everything, but we were all geared up and knew what had to be done. The only problem was publicizing it in so short a space of time. Fans had been ringing up the United reception for a while wanting to know when the testimonial game was taking place. We had already decided that the ticket prices would be pegged so that families and people who usually couldn't afford to come to Old Trafford could go. It was important to me that it should be a family night, an extended family night, if you see what I mean. There was also the chance for people to walk up to the gate and buy a ticket on the night. I said in interviews that it would be a return to earlier days when going to see United didn't require planning six weeks ahead. But afterwards I thought that even in 1987, when I first came to Old Trafford, crowds were 50,000 plus and hundreds were locked out.

Always lurking at the back of my mind was the thought that I'd be running out with Liam saying to me, "Why's there nobody here, Dad?" It was quite nerve-wracking. By the day before the game, we were really happy with the number of tickets we had sold, both in Scotland and here. We were looking at a crowd of between 20,000 and 25,000 and that seemed excellent to all of us.

The press were all very good about publicity: ITV even mentioned it during the Dortmund game coverage. The same was true after the game, when there was very little criticism of the amount of money the match had generated for someone who has been well-paid for ten years or so, as I have. Testimonials are becoming more and more controversial, and it's impossible to say anything in their defence without sounding a complete hypocrite. I'm frequently asked by fans if I think players' wages are too high. Well, you do have to qualify any question like that immediately by pointing out that the majority of professional footballers are not very well paid at all. You could also, with some justice, point to the enormous amount of revenue that players at the top generate for the clubs they play for, and stress the uncertainties of the profession. One minute you can be doing very nicely indeed, the next you can be stretchered off with your playing days over. That can happen at any time, even in a practice game. But, of course, that hasn't yet happened to me. If I wasn't so personally involved, and someone asked me if I thought top footballers were paid too much, I would say yes. On the other hand, I'm going to take what is offered me as a wage, for the sake of the future and for my family.

Over time, the justification for testimonials like mine has become less compelling. When footballers were paid low wages, testimonials provided them with a sum of money to give them a start after hanging up their boots. I have actually played for this club for ten years, which is a qualification of sorts beyond the ordinary, but I can't say I've been scraping a hand-to-mouth existence in that time. I tried to provide events that were value for money during the year and it was up to individuals whether to support them or not. All I can say is that I am hugely grateful to those who did.

The change in date for the testimonial match didn't just cause problems for the organizers. Two friends of mine that I used to play golf with in Scotland, Peter and Brian, were affected too. Brian phoned me to say that he had booked a family holiday and would have to go through with it. He had chosen April as he thought it would be a safe bet. So here he was, about to leave the country the only time that Celtic were playing United on behalf of his friend who had appeared for both.

"I can't come," he complained

"There's only one thing for it," I told him. "You'll have to cancel your holiday!"

"Oh, no, I can't!"

To compound his agony, Peter had rung him beforehand to tell him that he had been asked to take part in an exhibition game preceding the main match on the night, and that the Lisbon Lions would also be participating. I was about to put the phone down when he cried out,

"It's not true about the game with the Lisbon Lions is it? Tell me it's not true."

"Oh, Brian," I commiserated. "I'm terribly sorry. We had you pencilled in for that as well, but as you're going to be away..." I worked out that Peter was playing a particularly cruel practical joke – and, after thinking about putting him out of his misery for a second or two, decided against it and joined in. We let him go off thinking that one of the biggest nights of his life had just passed him by. Not only that, he would have to endure years of Peter reliving how wonderful it had been to be sharing a pitch with the victors of that memorable night in Portugal in 1967, when Celtic became the first British team to win the European Cup. I called Peter next and said,

"Look, Brian just told me what you'd said about the testimonial."

"Aye," he admitted, a bit shamefaced. "I did say that, it's true."

"Well, I agreed with you."

"Brilliant! I knew you'd catch on."

That's what friends are for...

On the day of the testimonial, I arrived at lunch time to sort out tickets for my family and friends. Maureen and my families had hired a coach down from Scotland, and it was late. On board was my granny, who would be celebrating her eighty-fifth birthday the next day. She had circumvented my Dad's attempts to stop her attending, thinking that the journey would have been too much for her. She wasn't having any of it. Granny told Dad that if he wouldn't let her on the bus she would find her own way down, and she would have done it, no problem. There was a Celtic supporter's coach organized from her village and she would have hitched a ride on that.

As the time of the match drew nearer, Maureen and I went to the Premier Lounge. It was set out so that we could have some food and a few drinks afterwards with our guests and make some presentations. There were several interviews for me to do. In one for Sky I described the Gaffer as a throat lozenge, "hard on the outside and soft and runny in the middle". Maybe I got a bit carried away with myself there. "Slightly softer in the middle" might be more accurate. The Gaffer also made an appearance to pay tribute to me, but he seemed to spend quite a long time going on about his mobile phone. As a joke I'd put a message on it, saying "Choccy is great!" As he is hopeless with anything technical, he couldn't remove it. He was convinced that, like me at the club, the message would be there forever, a thought too hideous for him to cope with. I also put an 0898 number on to the callback with the tag "Sexy Sadie". He was very puritanical about this. He missed the reference to the *White Album* and wouldn't try the number.

"Didn't you ring it back?" I asked him.

"Of course not," he replied, looking at me sternly in a "not what I expect from a father of three" way.

"It was only the *Daily Telegraph* crossword solution line," I informed him. A good joke wasted there, I'm afraid.

Our next job was to sort out the children. Liam was going to come out on to the pitch with me at the beginning, along with two other boys who had won competitions in the United programme. One was to accompany us out at the start and the other lad was to feature in a penalty shoot out competition at half-time. We got another couple of boys we knew to make up the numbers and one of them, who was from Airdrie, had to carry the enormous pressure of representing Scotland at this level. His Celtic strip evoked deafening cheers but, despite the vocal encouragement, the burden of bearing the hopes of a nation was just too much. He managed to miss every single one of his penalty kicks, spooning them over the bar. I've been there, missing penalties in front of even bigger crowds. He sent me a card afterwards saying how much he enjoyed taking part, so hopefully there won't be any lasting trauma.

The players began to arrive. The Gaffer had told everyone in the United squad to come as he didn't know who he was going to pick. Celtic had brought their stars, Paolo Di Canio and Jorge Cadete among them. We went to the dressing room and, after another three minutes moaning about his phone, pressing every button, and finding he couldn't remove the message, the Gaffer went through the team. It was a relief that I was actually starting this one, not on the bench. What would I have told Granny? I said to Kiddo, "I bet you told him to name the team without me in it," and Kiddo admitted that this was indeed the case. The Gaffer broke off from grousing about his phone for long enought to remind us that we needn't think that we were going to be strolling around for the evening. Celtic do not play friendlies, but matches, whatever the occasion. This is an attitude that the Gaffer fully endorses. He wished us good luck and a good game and smiled as we all left.

By this time the excitement was too much for my children to bear, especially Liam. He was dressed in the white United change strip and was ready to come out with me on to the pitch. He was supposed to carry the pennant. "Can we go out now, Dad?" was his constant refrain. When we were getting ready he asked me every few seconds if it was time to start. You can imagine his impatience when Graham, one of the three testimonial committee members who had worked so hard this year, came in to tell me that it was pandemonium outside. So many had turned up on the night, Celtic as well as Manchester United supporters, that the small number of turnstiles opened for the evening couldn't cope. The queues stretched right the way round the outside of the stadium. There was nothing we could do but delay the start of the game; we had to let in the crowds of people one way or another. The time moved on: 8.05, 8.20, 8.25, with Liam reminding me every few seconds. When we reached 8.20 we had to begin or people who had travelled hundreds of miles would be late back. Liam was also at the end of his tether.

"Here you are, son," I said as I tried to hand him the red commemorative pennant but he refused.

"I'm not having that," he answered, mulishly, "I'm taking the ball."

I sighed. I wasn't going to argue with him. The stress was taking its toll on both of us, and he is only five years old, after all. So we walked out together.

I'd already been into the stadium once to receive a super presentation from the Disabled Supporters' Association. I was very moved by their kind regards, a splendid beginning to the evening. I'd seen then that there was a fair-sized crowd, but the seats were far from full and I wasn't prepared for what I saw as I came out through the traditional lines of players from both teams on to the pitch. There were so many people. The cheering, particularly from the Celtic fans who made sure that there was a tremendous atmosphere, was deafening. For a moment I felt overwhelmed with emotion, and had to fight hard to regain my composure. I remember thinking that I should take everything in so I could carry it all away with me. I would never experience anything like it again. You never know how many people will come to a testimonial anyway, but I must admit that I wondered how many would come to mine. I've become used to hearing very little that is positive when I come on during games. That's the supporters' prerogative. It's natural, I suppose, for people to focus on the negative aspects of your play, and abuse can be funny and part of the enjoyment fans get out of football. But a testimonial is a very public and large-scale test of people's attitude towards you. Some shreds of my ego still remain and can be delicate on occasions. You have to be a realist and say that it was a beautifully sunny evening, and there are always thousands who want to come and watch United and Celtic, but the numbers there gave me a very warm feeling.

I had to hold the pennant in my teeth to applaud everyone as Liam had trotted out with the ball, which made an interesting, if undignified photograph for the album. Then I had to work hard to persuade him to kick the ball to me, which he did very carefully with the fierce deliberation of small children who want to get everything right. The game itself was over far too quickly for me. We took the lead through a goal from Roy Keane but Celtic did indeed play hard. Several times I was on the end of a crunching tackle which demonstrated their approach. At half-time, most of our first-teamers were replaced by Reserves and Celtic scored twice to end up 2–1 winners.

At the finish, I went to get Liam and the girls to walk round the pitch with me. Liam capped his evening by bursting into tears, sobbing loudly.

"What's the matter now?" I asked him.

"We got beat!" he lamented, inconsolable for a few minutes. When we were walking round I noticed something else was wrong.

"Liam, why aren't you waving to anyone?"

"There's too many people, Dad." Naturally, I didn't agree with him.

My children were to wear three different strips: Manchester United's white away kit and the blue third kit (the one that resembles the Rangers' kit), and a Celtic strip to make up the trio of outfits. Laura agreed to wear the Celtic kit, without much enthusiasm, but of course as we made our circuit of the pitch she got the loudest cheer from the Celtic end. Afterwards she wouldn't take the strip off and now she wears it as pyjamas. I am very pleased that we have a Celtic fan in the making here. Siobhan took to the limelight like a natural, waving and loving every minute of it.

When we had finished I went to do the press interviews. I couldn't help noticing how white Tommy Burns's hair had turned from the fiery red it was when I played alongside him at Celtic. It probably whitened still further over the next couple of weeks, when Celtic departed from the Scottish Cup in the semi finals, knocked out in the replay by Falkirk. I imagine it's gone back to red since he lost the managership of the club and the stress that goes with it. I met him just before he was given

1997, Testimonial Gala Ball: Brian and Maureen McClair.

15 April 1997, Old Trafford: "There's too many people, Dad."

"Laura agreed to wear the Celtic kit without much enthusiasm, but of course as we made our circuit of the pitch she got the loudest cheer from the Celtic fans. Now she wears it as pyjamas."

"I had to hold the pennant in my teeth to applaud... an interesting if undignified photograph for the album."

"And if you know your history, it's enough to make your heart go woah-oh-oh!"

19 April 1997, Anfield: Liverpool 1, Manchester United 3. "The corners drill was the brainwave of our coaching supremo – or rather, it was Kiddo's masterstroke until we scored two goals from corners and then it was the Gaffer's idea."

23 April 1997, Old Trafford: Manchester United 0, Borussia Dortmund 1. "We had twenty shots... I've never seen a team defend like Dortmund for so long and be fortunate enough to keep us out for the whole match."

"The younger players managed to lift themselves much more easily than the older ones, who had grown to believe that the trophy was within reach."

11 May 1997, Old Trafford, with Jim Ryan. "I used to stay at the back and act cool, as if I could take it or leave it. Now I just want to be to the fore in all the photographs. Sod dignity."

"I'm more than happy to be sweating it out with the rest."

1 October 1997, Old Trafford: Manchester United 3, Juventus 0. "Talented sports people can usually achieve a high level of performance but they have occasions when, for some reason, they go beyond that."

25 October 1997, Old Trafford: Manchester United 7, Barnsley 0. "In the Premier League we have finally discovered the knack of winning games by a large margin."

10 December 1997, Stadio Delle Alpi: Juventus 1, Manchester United 0. "It would have been better for us to have secured their exit in the final game by beating them."

Andy Cole: "As soon as he was fit enough to play with the sharpness and acceleration his type of game demands, the goals flowed."

24 January 1998, Old Trafford: Manchester United 5, Walsall 1. "The shocking sight of Brian McClair playing for the whole of a first team game."

"What a privilege it is to be associated with a club like this one."

the job. For some reason I was at Manchester Airport, and I saw Tommy walking towards me dressed in flip-flops, the brightest T-shirt I had ever seen and shorts. Nothing unusual you might think, but it was absolutely freezing.

"Hiya, Tommy," I greeted him, breezily, "You been offered the job?"

"Oh, no, no, no." He was very keen, over-keen really, to deny everything.

"Where's the family?" I looked around.

"All still out there on holiday."

"Aye," I said, knowingly. "Well, all the best then. I hope you enjoy it."

By all accounts he was taken to a hotel in Manchester to discuss terms. Like Kenny Dalglish said when he was offered the Newcastle job, an offer to manage Celtic must be something you think deeply about accepting – for all of one second.

The final task of the evening was to distribute presents. It is customary to give players something for taking part in the game and I'd been thinking for some time about what it should be. It's standard to present them with crystal, and you can accumulate a fair amount in your time as a player. I wasn't sure that younger, unmarried players would quite know what to do with it. We have been given electronic personal organizers, but not everyone understands how to use them. I was very proud of my idea of giving everyone a Discman. Unfortunately, Bryan Gunn had got there before me, and he had distributed them to the teams which followed the dog show in his testimonial earlier on in the season. I gave them a Discman each anyway because I'd already bought them.

Though it's difficult to believe that a large group of Scots could congregate on an evening like this without a party, there was no celebration as the family were all going straight back on their coach to Scotland. Many of them were at work the next morning. My brother drove down by car, as his wife had given birth to their first child the day before. Pictures were taken, photographs signed and everyone had gone before midnight. The kids were still hyper though, so when we finally reached home we watched part of the video Kath Phipps, from reception, had organized so that Liam could see himself coming on to the pitch and the girls could watch themselves going round at the end. After that we managed to get them into bed. The papers next day had some excellent photographs and write-ups, though in several of them my status as one of football's Renaissance men was confirmed in captions describing me as "Brain McClair". The testimonial committee was thrilled by the success of its efforts. Graham isn't even a United supporter; he follows West Ham and Manchester City. He walked round announcing, "Four, three, four, three, seven... Unbelievable!" The final attendance figure, 43,437, said it all, really. It's a reminder, if one were needed, of what football means to people. And afterwards I went to my post and found that some fans who couldn't attend sent me money instead. You can imagine how that made me feel.

Maureen read something out to me from the programme at the end, saying it summed me up exactly. John Colquhoun had described me as "still the most awkward, argumentative, twisted footballer I have had the pleasure to call my friend."

13

This time on Merseyside

"Who needs virtual reality?"

This is the bit in any book where, with the supreme benefit bestowed by hindsight, you can look back and pronounce, "This was the turning point".

After the important business of my testimonial, we were to face Liverpool on Saturday 19 April with an early kick-off. It was one of those matches dubbed "the Championship decider" – usually by Sky, because they have exclusive live coverage. This time, though, the match lived up to the hype. At the time we had no way of knowing how crucial it was going to be, for we were still in the European competition. When we were eliminated from the Champions' League four days after the Anfield tie, it began to be clear how important the result of this game was.

Every game now was vital. But that has been the case for the last six seasons at this club. We had played forty-eight games in four competitions, and each of those forty-eight results was highly significant. Add to this the international games that some of our number had been playing, and the level of pressure on individuals is obvious. Personally, this was the first match against Liverpool at Anfield since I've been at the club that I didn't start. In the nine games there in my time we've only won once and been royally gubbed on several occasions.

There had been no special training beforehand in preparation. We had spent a wee bit of time practising corners, which is something we rarely do. The corners drill was the brainwave of our coaching supremo – or rather, it was Kiddo's masterstroke until we scored two goals from corners in the match and then it became the Gaffer's idea. We must have devoted all of five minutes to it in training, all waiting together, then when the ball was crossed running in different directions. It was hardly the master plan that it became in the post-match conference. Players at this level are so good you don't have to spend hours putting them through a training move. You just say to them, "Look, you – deliver the ball here, and you – run that way," and that is more than sufficient explanation. Of course, they may not always remember to do it.

We stayed in a hotel overnight despite not having far to travel. We tend to do this if we play Liverpool, but the Gaffer and Kiddo were also concerned that all our energies should be focused in the last four weeks of the season.

The team took ten minutes to settle down at the start of the game, by which time Kiddo had screamed himself hoarse on the bench. The atmosphere was terrific, owing much to the great empathy there is between Liverpool and United's fans. But then we took the lead. Beckham put in a great corner, our players ran in different directions as per instructions, and Pally rose to meet the ball. He has probably never headed the ball so well in his life. He used to look as if his forehead was made of putty when it came to offensive, rather than defensive headers, but this time the ball shot off his head with force and found its mark. But our dream start was quickly cancelled out, and it was disappointing to allow Liverpool back in the game from an equalizer which was purely the result of not organizing ourselves fast enough. Before the game we'd spoken about marshalling ourselves immediately to deal with short corners, but we didn't do it. A fine cross found its way onto the head of John Barnes, who showed that he hasn't lost his skill in the air. To see him score must have been particularly galling for the Gaffer who had made a point of reminding us in the team talk that Barnes was a good header of the ball. And we were all listening so intently.

Liverpool came back into the game after that, and had a spell where they asserted themselves. Robbie Fowler was lively without posing any direct threat. Once again the corner master strategy came to our aid when Pally, running in a different direction from everyone else, jumped and put in another tremendous header. I had to pinch myself on the bench to check that I wasn't hallucinating. Two headed goals from corners, at Anfield, and from Gary Pallister!

It would be impossible to talk about this game without mentioning the problems David James had in goal. He did appear at fault for our second, though you couldn't really blame him for our first goal which would have been difficult for anyone to stop. Andy Cole had a chance to send us in at half-time with a 3–1 lead, but he didn't realize how much time he had, and we had to settle for the 2–1 scoreline – with which we were delighted.

In the second half we added a further goal to our lead and, as it turned out, we could have won by a far larger margin. Gary Neville did well to beat his man but the cross he sent over was not particularly well judged. That didn't matter, as the goalkeeper missed the ball, it hit Coley in the ear and rolled over the line. Later, Andy had a further gilt-edged opportunity but didn't want to be too greedy as we had already wrapped up the game. Reluctant because of past experiences to begin chicken-counting at all, when the final whistle blew I still felt it was the sort of performance that boded a fourth Championship in five years. And we were finished by 1.15 pm. It was like getting an extra day's holiday.

Once again, I picked up the newspapers on a Sunday and discovered Manchester United had been involved in a serious incident which had escaped our attention. Perhaps there really is a parallel universe in which other possibilities are played out. Our coach, I read with interest, was supposed to have been pelted with missiles. Apparently we had to run a gauntlet of "abuse and hate". There have undoubtedly been times in the past when it's been a bit lively as we've got on and off our coach at Anfield. Signing autographs and having them torn up immediately in your face is a favourite, but it hardly reduces us to tears. In fact, it makes me laugh. It seems an appropriate judgment on their worth. There is usually some humour to add spice to the situation too. You have to accept that if you win a game with so much at stake, maybe even the Championship, opposition fans want to try and hit back in some way, and that is likely to be in the form of ferocious barracking.

Following the bomb scare and security alert at the Grand National, we had been told that if a similar thing happened at the Anfield game we would be evacuated from the ground immediately. So we made arrangements to walk across the car park to the bus, and we deposited all our car keys in the trustworthy hands of Albert. If the alarm had gone while we were playing we wouldn't have been allowed to go back to the dressing rooms to pick up car keys until the Monday. At the end of the game these arrangements were still in place, so we walked across the pitch and out through the back way across to the coach. Some Liverpool fans spotted us, and there were a few comments made, but on the whole it was good natured. I was asked some questions by a journalist from the *Daily Mirror* and amused myself by adopting the politician's technique of answering a completely different one from the one asked.

As we boarded the bus, the Liverpool stewards were fantastic and a credit to their club. Not only did they praise us for our performance, they also moved a bloke off straight away who was getting abusive. An object did wing its way over at this point, but it was a cardboard chip carton, closely followed by a paper cup. "Whoops!" said I, "That could have been really nasty. Someone could have picked up a deep paper gash from one of those." Then a styrofoam cup of coffee made contact with the windscreen. There was a grave danger, considering the chemical properties of most beverages served at football grounds, that it would melt through the glass.

Punctuated by our elimination against Dortmund, there were eleven days before our next Premier League game against Leicester on Saturday 3 May at Filbert Street. It was the first of the run of four matches in nine days which took us to the end of the season. Everyone seemed to expect that we would have the Championship more or less sewn up by the end of the day – everyone outside our dressing room, that is. We knew it was going to be a very hard game, particularly as Leicester City still needed points to be safe. We travelled down to the Midlands on the Friday and it was so hot on the bus we were allowed to loosen the collars of our smart shirts. The forecast had said that the weather was about to break, probably by the Saturday morning on which the game was to take place. Even if the hot weather held up it was logical to expect that the early kick-off time would ensure that we would be playing in relatively cool temperatures at that part of the day. Another theory shattered: it was absolutely sweltering and airless. It was too hot for me even to be a substitute, perhaps because Kiddo and the Gaffer thought there'd be a greater danger of me melting.

It wasn't only the weather which we couldn't control. Our defending went haywire too. "What are we doing here? What the **** is going on?" was the verdict from the bench on both goals that we gave away in the first half. Philosophy came to my aid. It wouldn't be a Manchester United run-in for the title if we weren't busy making it as difficult as possible for ourselves, would it? The one spark of consolation was that, in between our woefully disorganized defensive play, we'd created some good chances – but then so had Leicester City. There is no doubt that Leicester could have scored several more goals, all from our lapses of concentration and failure to organize. It may be arrogance, or maybe we are genuinely so fit that we can finish a game stronger than any other team in the Premier League. In any event, we always believe that we can come back from behind. When we scored just before half-time, we were convinced we could go on to win.

United did dominate the second half, thanks mainly to a tremendous performance from Andy Cole. Certainly Solskjaer benefited from his hard work. We felt that we might even have won it in the last fifteen or twenty minutes. After the match we tried to console ourselves. We moaned about the heat, how hard the pitch was, what a difficult game it had been, how much Leicester had needed the points and so on. We even threw in the one about how everyone wants to lift themselves when they are playing against us. Oh yes, and the one about how early in the morning it was (note the convenient amnesia about our victory at Anfield after an 11.15 kick-off). By the time we'd finished running through that litany of excuses, we were more or less satisfied with the single point we'd earned. None of these factors applied to Leicester, of course. I think the team was definitely weary, even the players who didn't play in the mid-week internationals. Gary Pallister, Nicky Butt and Phil Neville had not turned out for England against Italy but they were still tired. I don't know what sort of training they underwent in the England camp, but it was a long time to be away. Some of the other internationals, like Solskjaer, had had to travel; but it was the ones who hadn't travelled far who were exhausted.

When Brian Kidd has us all gathered together here, we work hard and get through a great deal of work, but not at the expense of our stamina. Perhaps when you fit into a different training structure, with coaches looking forward to a completely different game, it works against the routine you are used to.

Though United's players were tired at this stage of the season because of the number of matches some had played, we had been in this sort of situation many times. We know what to expect when the really unbearable pressure is on at the end of the season. Even the younger players have, by and large, gone through it once. We know what it takes just to be in contention for Championships, let alone win them. Brian Kidd's training schedules are designed so that we have the reserves of stamina to be ready at the finish. The structure of the whole season is considered, not just any one part of it. The coaches here expect that, as long as we have a reasonable break in the summer, we'll last out to the end and come on stronger. Though the management were still pressing for an extension to the season, those involved with preparing the players were ignoring that possibility. United were ready to take on the sort of compressed fixture list that awaited them.

Mental strain is usually dismissed by people who haven't gone through it, but the team was coping well and no one had got to the stage where they weren't sleeping well the night before a match. Part of the support team's job is to try to take away as much anxiety as they can, to impress players with how everything has been laid out for them and every contingency covered, even if it hasn't. With the madness that descends on the last few fixtures of the season, if you are looking to win something or gain a place in Europe, or avoid relegation, there needs to be a feeling that it is somehow all under control and going according to plan. Only the wealthiest clubs have the resources to do this.

As an illustration, rather than let us go home after the Leicester fixture, the team was taken to a hotel in Cheshire which was, frustratingly, only a few minutes away from my home. The sentries were out to make sure that the Cheshire dwellers didn't sneak away in the night. The idea behind this was that we needed a proper rest and if we went home then that just wouldn't happen. The only way to be certain that the players would do absolutely nothing but relax and sleep was to take us away to a place where we would have no option but to have a meal, watch television and go to bed early. If they went home, family men wouldn't just lie around on the sofa, as there would be children to play with and rubbish to be put out and the hundred and one other things that wives are left to struggle with on their own when we are away. When we awoke in the morning we went to a short training session and were allowed to return home after lunch, refreshed and rested under the eagle eye of the Gaffer and Kiddo.

In contrast to the baking heat of the Leicester game, we were plunged into stormy and wet conditions for the Monday game against Middlesbrough. Wet is an understatement; the rain belted down and the wind was relentless. If Leicester had still needed the points to be sure of avoiding relegation, Middlesbrough were absolutely desperate. Many people other than myself have commented on what an anomaly it was that a team which had such inspired and talented individuals found itself in that position. On their day, there is no doubt that they could sweep aside the best. But, in the end, there was a lack of resistance about their defending. We'd seen them take leads but not know how to hang on to them. This was a fortunate weakness from our point of view and we would reap full benefit from it in this match.

In the team talk, the Gaffer sang the praises of Juninho and how he could do anything with a football if he was allowed to play. This must have wetted the appetite of our players to witness his Brazilian magic at first hand, as we gave him the freedom of Manchester to really turn it on. He didn't disappoint. I know that many clubs made the decision to man-mark him to keep him out of the game, but that isn't the way Manchester United play. Anyway, I don't think we have a player that we could have assigned to that role. Perhaps Roy Keane would have been the one we could have selected for that purpose. But if you had tied Roy up in that way so much else would have been missing from our own game. We need the contribution he makes in the midfield to play at our best. Instead you would expect that United will be organized enough to pick Juninho up throughout the game anyway, so our particular tactics should not have made a difference. Nobody had explained that to Juninho, perhaps because of the language barrier, and he ran us all over the place in the first half and scored a lovely first goal. We came back into the game with an equalizer from Roy Keane, but two minutes later we were 3–1 down. Again, as against Leicester, it was the goal we pulled back before half-time that was our way back into the game. It was fitting that it was a superb strike from Gary Neville – his first ever goal for the club.

At 3–2 we believed that we could go on to win. There had been five goals in the first half and there was nothing to say that there couldn't be even more in the second. Although we equalized and there were loud calls for a penalty at the end (the loudest of all from the Gaffer, admittedly), we only earned a point. However, once again there was a rational explanation for it all. The weather was terrible and didn't relent. There were great pools of standing water in the middle of the pitch by the end of the match, which were stopping the ball dead. I remarked jocularly to the groundsman as the downpour showed no signs of abating, "I don't think you should have watered the pitch beforehand!" As we had come back from 3–1 down, we could always feel that we had won a point rather than let two slip. The manager remarked afterwards that it was the worst defending he had seen at the club in the last six years. Well, his memory is very short. He's not going to convince me that the defending in the 5–0 defeat by Newcastle and the 6–3 against Southampton was better than that!

After the match we watched a little bit of Liverpool's game against Tottenham Hotspur. We firmly expected Liverpool to steamroller Spurs, even without Fowler, who was suspended after being sent off and who is arguably their most influential player. But although they won by two goals to one, what I saw of their performance made me feel quietly confident. The more I watched, the more I was convinced that Liverpool, our closest challengers, didn't believe they could still go on to win the League. Maybe it was just wishful thinking on my part, but I definitely got that impression. Our nearest rivals all had very difficult games to play in their run up. United can testify to how Wimbledon will give you absolutely nothing and how much they love that sort of occasion. And as for West Ham, this time they needed the points to ensure they safely avoided relegation. Having our two fixtures at home in such close proximity actually benefited us, in that the spotlight, and the pressure, fell back on Newcastle and Liverpool. If we had lost either of those two games maybe it would have been different, but we fought back. Both our rivals now had to go out and get a result to secure their own success, rather than wait for us to fail. They could not afford to drop points themselves. If Liverpool lost and Newcastle failed to take all three points from their matches, United would win the Premier League.

I sat down to watch the Newcastle versus West Ham game on television having bathed Liam, and he settled down with me on the sofa.

"Who do you want to win, Dad?" said a little voice after a minute.

"West Ham, son," I told him.

"Oh," he replied, and went quiet as he thought about that for a bit.

"What's the matter, Liam?"

"I want Newcastle to win, Dad." He likes Alan Shearer.

Eventually I persuaded him round to my way of thinking, or so I thought.

We watched quietly together for all of twenty minutes, then the strain began to tell on one of us. I started to flick to the Liverpool score on teletext. This gave me a headache, so I toyed with the idea of turning on the live commentary on Radio 5. A few seconds of this torment told me I couldn't cope with it, and I switched it off. Liam stared at me as if to say, "Why are you doing this to yourself, Dad?" Now left watching only one game, as the tie wore on and the score remained 0–0, I started to shout at the television. I ended up bellowing when Newcastle won a corner, even though they had put the ball out.

"That's it! Newcastle are going to score here, I just know it, because it's definitely not a corner, and that's always the way!" I thundered. Who needs virtual reality?

"Will Shearer score, Dad?" Liam asked hopefully.

Miklosko briefly became my favourite goalkeeper by pulling off a great save from the corner-which-wasn't. Then suddenly it was all over, and Manchester United were Premier League Champions again, for the fourth time in five years. I would win the League from the sofa in my house every time, if I had the chance. Forget about the romantic view that it would be nice to win it out on the pitch, at home, in front of our own fans. Forget having to go through another nerve-wracking ninety minutes. Any kind of win will do. Liam was very happy too, though I still think he was secretly disappointed that Alan Shearer wasn't on the score sheet.

The next day at training we posed for photographs and were expected to spray ourselves wastefully with champagne for the benefit of the cameras. Otherwise, our job was to prepare for the two games that still remained and which were both sell-outs. The match against Newcastle on Thursday 8 May was not, therefore, yet another Championship decider; we had not kept our fans on the edge of their seats until the very last game. The big frisson for all our supporters were the wild rumours circulating that Peter Schmeichel was going to play centre forward and would be taking the penalties. Loads of people asked me about it. Several others told me it was "a fact" when I denied it. The source of the story appeared to be a clip on the Manchester United Video Magazine, in which the Gaffer complimented Peter on the excellence of his injury-time "goal" against Wimbledon in the Cup. He said he had promised Peter that if we had won the Championship by the last match, he would let him go up front... maybe. Of course, there was never any possibility that would happen. We had to approach both our last two fixtures in a thoroughly professional manner, as the outcomes of both games would affect European places and might influence the relegation fight. It wouldn't have been fair on Arsenal or Liverpool, no matter what the fans would like to see. Who knows if we might be in a similar situation next year, in second place and depending upon the League Champions, whoever they might be, to defeat our closest challengers so we can qualify for the second Champions' League place? What if Peter broke his leg? The manager had only one thing in mind in his preparations, and that was winning the game and winning it well. So we approached it no differently to any other tie. He said to us beforehand, "We've lost thirty League games in six years, and we don't want the total to rise to thirty this season." He always has his eye on things like that.

Everything seemed to be proceeding smoothly in the game, which was accompanied by the song "Schmeichel up front", until eight minutes after kick-off when Kiddo told me to go and warm up as Roy Keane had signalled that he had a problem. It was so muddy along the sidelines that I couldn't run up and down without my feet slipping from underneath me – it was a quagmire. A glance along the bench told me that the Gaffer wouldn't play either Solskjaer or Cole in that position, so it was going to be me who came on for the last eighty minutes. I must have had a premonition that I might have had a greater involvement in this game, as I had gone for a nap in the afternoon as part of my preparations (well, that was the excuse I gave). However, it was later pointed out to me that my pre-match warm-up had consisted solely of having a discussion with Brian Kidd in the centre circle. I hadn't done any shooting as I usually do, thus ensuring the safety of the spectators behind the goal. My first action was to put in a superb tackle on Alan Shearer just outside the box on the right, coming away with the ball and congratulating myself on my timing. Then I heard the whistle. The referee, to my amazement, had blown for a foul. I could not believe that I had been penalized for such a fine bit of play.

I thought I played well in this game, in fact, I had independent confirmation of this while taking a throw in. Someone shouted, "Newcastle, you're ***** [ie no good]. Even Choccy's having a blinder!" It was a pity that we couldn't score, as we had plenty of chances. I played a very good through ball to Andy Cole which nearly did put us in front. I would say that it's something of a skill to scoop the ball up near your own shoulder and then turn and pull the opposing centre forward down, winning a free kick in the process, as Srnicek did. I don't really see how that works. The referee has to give what he sees, but I'd like to know how he managed to see that particular incident in that way.

In the second half, tiredness crept in and we definitely defended too deep. Newcastle began to create a few chances, but they hardly looked like a team who needed points to get into the Champions' League. David May thought they might need a hand and did his best to give them the lead. Peter Schmeichel was shouting at him to leave the ball, but it was in a very dangerous position with Newcastle forwards bearing down on it. I thought that bit of advice from our goalkeeper wasn't terribly helpful. "I hope he doesn't decide to leave it," was the thought that ran through my mind. Maysie was of the same opinion, but then he got to the ball and it looked very much as if it was going to end up in the back of his own net. In the end his intervention spun off the post, and only the camber of the pitch took it away a fraction and spared his blushes.

At the finish it remained 0–0, but I was baffled when I noticed that players were swapping shirts. Why? It wasn't the last game of the season, nor was it a cup tie. "I'm not swapping shirts with any Newcastle player wearing that away kit," I decided. Maybe if it had been their striped kit I might have been tempted, but not the blue and grey monstrosity. When someone asked me I said, "No, sorry, I can't. It doesn't belong to me," which strictly it doesn't.

This reminded me of when I first came to United and felt the lash of the manager's tongue over my profligacy with a red shirt. At Celtic you used to get strips all the time and frequently used to swap them, at European games and Cup finals of course, but at other times too. Anyway, one of the first games I played after signing for United was in a League of Ireland match, and one of the Irish players at the end asked me if I would swap shirts. I didn't think twice about doing it, as for him it was a special game and you could understand why he would want a souvenir. However, our performance in the match was completely awful and, even though it was only a friendly, to the manager it was a game like any other. In his eyes we had let ourselves down and had failed to follow his instructions. No matter whether it had been a Cup final or an exhibition match, he wanted you to play the way he had told you. If you didn't, he would let you know about it, and he certainly did on this occasion. It was my first real view of what Alex Ferguson could be like if things didn't go his way. He turned to me, his new signing, and gave me an absolute rocket for swapping my shirt, which he informed me you just did not do at Manchester United unless it was the final of the European Cup, and even then I should think very hard about it.

I was excruciatingly embarrassed and thought for several terrible moments that he was going to send me to ask for my shirt back. He was probably considering it. So at the Newcastle match, I swapped my shirt with Paul Scholes and got a nice red one in exchange. I discovered on a trip to the Old Trafford laundry with my children, when I was showing them how a football club worked, that each player is expected to get through the season with two shirts of each colour (but not if you give them away), and there is a sewing machine for mending them if they are torn. This doesn't include the special shirts made for Europe. Jordi Cruyff wanted to keep his strip for every single game he played this season. This is what would happen at Barcelona, where they have a new shirt every game. Then he realized what paupers Manchester United were compared with the Spanish team.

The other thing I discovered on my trip to the laundry, which was something I knew already, is that Manchester United is kept going by a large number of dedicated staff who work very hard in the service of the club. They certainly don't consider it just a job. As I said in an earlier chapter, players are very often blissfully unaware of the whole of the business that is Manchester United. The laundry is round by the side of the Megastore and is a massive room with a high ceiling and walls of whitewashed breeze-block. It's noisy and it's hot and the women who work there arrive at 7.15 am to find seventy or eighty numbered sets of shirts, shorts, socks and jockstraps wrapped in numbered towels – the training kit – waiting for them. They load these into two huge fifty-pound washing machines and finish them in four giant industrial tumble driers by 11.15, have a short break, then the morning's load from the workout at the Cliff arrives. I was amazed to find out that as late as the end of the seventies the kit was only washed once a week. I don't think having to train in dirty kit would go down very well now.

My weans noticed the giant green-and-blue goalies' kits hanging from a line strung across part of the room to dry. The socks were enormous and made me laugh as they dangled down. They looked like items that would have belonged better in *Jack and the Beanstalk*. These outsized clothes aren't dried in the driers in case they shrink. Apparently, goalkeepers are such big men that the kits barely fit; any shrinkage would be disastrous! They even wash the flags here. We players just expect that it will be all laid out for us in neat piles, set out by Albert. We would only notice if it was missing. The manager, though, frequently visits the laundry, going into the little staff room there to eat his spartan breakfast (one piece of toast, one cup of tea and one Weetabix) and read their copy of the paper if he is at Old Trafford early on a nontraining day.

After the Newcastle game, when I staggered to the players' lounge, people were most concerned about my welfare as I had played virtually the whole game. Kiddo started off the hilarity by dubbing me "Juninho", then my wife decided to join in by offering to go and get me the wheelchair. It wasn't my legs that were troubling me; they were holding up well. my face, however, felt distinctly odd. In a Roald Dahl kind of way it appeared to have swollen up during the game and was incredibly sore. Maureen said that I was looking a bit strange and on closer investigation in the mirror, I saw that my face had puffed up and turned bright red. It was probably sunburn, or maybe fatigue burn, as I have very fair skin which could get sunburnt at night. A journalist recently described me as "swarthy", which the dictionary defines as "dark skinned", but I think the epithet he was searching for was "unshaven". Still, even though I survived the game reasonably well, I was too tired to go to the celebration of our Premier League win afterwards and though Maureen and I said we would drop in on our way home, we decided to give it a miss.

Early next day I was at Old Trafford waiting for Gary Neville, who had foolishly arranged the day before to meet me there. He had made it to the evening celebration. As a result of my procrastination, I wasn't going to be able to pay everyone from the players' pool. Every team has a players' pool, where any small amounts of money earned for interviews are paid into a central fund and then shared out at the close of the season. This is meant to prevent the "stars" of the moment monopolizing the interviews and profiting unfairly at the expense of the rest of the team. Each cheque paying money out of the pool has to have two signatories. The co-signatory along with myself used to be Steve Bruce. In fact, it had been Steve Bruce all the way through this season as well, even though he's been at Birmingham for a wee while now. Before he left, I had him sign a whole book of cheques just to tide me over. I hadn't done anything else about it until the signed cheques ran out this week and it became necessary for me to find another co-signatory, preferably one who actually played for the team.

I arranged to go to the bank and sort it out so that Gary Neville, that very responsible young man, could be the second signatory. However, I received a phone call from Phil at about half ten telling me that Gary hadn't got out of bed yet. I suggested it was because his sister had hidden the ladder of their bunk beds, but Phil assured me that

Gary was still asleep. "Not to worry," I said, "I'm sure he's very... tired."

Gary had a sore leg to go with his sore head. I didn't see John Beresford's challenge, but he had a hole in his right shin pad which he paraded dramatically after the game for us all to see, and a matching hole in his shin which required two stitches. There was an amusing side to his injury, not for Gary, but for the rest of us. He was so involved in the game that it took him quite a while to realize that he had been hurt. There was a gap of at least two minutes before you saw him react, as if he suddenly said to himself, "Ahh, pain! I'd better do something about it!" I didn't see his retaliation where he pushed Beresford over as I was following the ball. I only saw the usual gaggle of players that gather when an incident has occurred. At least abusing John Beresford gave the United fans some variation from baiting Alan Shearer, their main victim for virtually the whole of the match.

So I missed Gary, but as the reward of virtue I found a gift in my post, a Tamagotchi electronic pet from Japan. I'd mentioned them in the Diary some months before. I am attached to it already. I have high hopes that the subliminal messages I've placed in previous installments which say "Rolex" and "Porsche" will bear fruit any day now. Seriously, though, I went into a shop in Manchester where the star of a children's show was trying to use his celebrity status to extort free goods from the assistants. He asked me what I'd had free as a footballer and I told him, "Verbal abuse!" He left very quickly after that.

14

After the ball

"I am not a hat person."

Our final celebration of the season was to be on Sunday 11 May when West Ham came to Old Trafford. However, it wasn't just the first team which came to the party. By some freak coincidence, the Reserves, the A team and the B team had all won their respective Leagues too. We wanted to win the game as well, and the manager picked a team to do so. West Ham had stayed up in the Premiership and the pressure was off both teams. The papers had tried to generate some pressure of their own by saying that United must be worried by the team not winning a match at Old Trafford since March. This was a nonsensical distortion, as we had only played two home games in April, against Derby and Dortmund, and our three games in May were all crammed into the space of one week.

However, though we won comfortably 2–0, the football was really a prelude to the presentation. Spectators were able to witness a superb strike from Paul Scholes for the first goal, which Solskjaer followed up with a header. I had a look at the replay from the half-way line, and Paul had put it over. He can claim the goal with justice. I came on in the second half and exercised my football brain by making a magnificent run across the goal so that Eric could slot the ball to Jordi. The selfish thought did cross my mind that my Dutch team mate could have passed the ball to me so that I could have had a chance of scoring at least one first-team goal this season, but I dismissed this unworthy thought after a few hours. Jordi put it away with panache, just to underline the point.

Another part of the entertainment was the amount of stick that David Beckham took from the West Ham fans over his current domestic arrangements. He took the opportunity to drop down on to one knee when we'd scored. It was a strange celebration of a goal, almost as if he was proposing.

At the end of the game it was back to the dressing room for a short break and then out again to the pomp and circumstance. Fans of other Premier League teams will probably not have noticed, never having the need for the song, but singing along with the Queen version of "We are the Champions" causes people who aren't opera singers enormous problems. At one point, the song changes key, and the whole crowd strains desperately for the notes, eyes watering. So as Old Trafford squealed along to this overplayed anthem and the other tunes on the karaoke tape of extracts from club songs, we made our way along the tunnel, not knowing what delights lay in store. There were some thin wooden doors over the mouth of the tunnel in black and silver with the Carling logo on them. They wobbled as we pushed them apart and strode into the light. My one aim was to get as close to the front as I could. In the old days, when my career stretched in front of me, I used to stay at the back and act cool, as if I could take it or leave it. Now I just want to be to the fore in all the photographs. Sod dignity.

On either side of the black and silver mat which had been rolled out was a guard of honour composed of the members of the three other League-winning United teams this year. The A team usually win their League but the B team hadn't won their particular trophy for a time, and they won it right at the end of the season by goal difference after a couple of great wins. The Reserves eventually stumbled over the line to win theirs. It was a good idea to organize things in this way, as every player could join in and feel part of the club's success. Everyone received their medals before a huge crowd – a reward to be savoured when you've been appearing in front of a few hundred, as is the case with the B team. I had successfully elbowed most of the first team out of the way so I was fourth in the line to raise the Premier League trophy on high and collect my medal. After lining up all together for a group photo, we set off on our victory parade around the pitch, keeping nicely within the touchlines so that we didn't spark off a pitch invasion. That would never do, would it?

My main aim, besides getting in some top-quality waving and applauding, was to stop myself putting on any silly hats. Maureen has left me in no doubt that I am not a hat person. In every celebration for many years, I've not been able to resist donning a bobble hat or flat cap and knotting a scarf like a muffler under my chin. But now I have been told, "Brian! Don't put on any more hats, you just look stupid!" So I had to fight down the overpowering urge. When we got back to the dressing room, Ken Merrett approached me and presented me with my Pontin's League medal. I didn't go out to collect it at half-time when the Reserves had their presentation, not because, as was announced, I was having my cup of tea, but because I thought one appearance from me would be quite enough for the crowd. I felt a great sense of satisfaction at having done my own particular version of the double again. You couldn't afford to blink in the crowd, as you might miss a presentation. Ken Doherty paraded with his World Snooker Championship trophy, Michael Clegg was named Reserve Team Player of the year and Eric received a trophy he had been awaiting for twelve months.

Eric's award was a miniature of the statue of Sir Matt Busby which stands proudly above the stadium forecourt. This statuette is now to be given to the Sir Matt Busby Player of the Year. Though no one said anything about it at the time, Eric seemed very preoccupied and slightly distanced from events, as though he was thinking very hard about something. He had been like that for a few weeks. But who knew just what was going on in his mind even at the best of times?

Now the season was over, it was also time to put the finish to my testimonial year. There were two final events. The first showed that people will make a television programme out of anything, even if it's a group of footballers playing mediocre golf in a gale. Manchester City and United players, present and past, were to take part in a tournament which was billed as the "Manchester Derby". Well, there wasn't one on the pitch this season and won't be one next, unless the Cup draws throw one up. The day was jointly organized by my own and Paul Lake's committee. Paul was a City player who snapped his cruciate ligament in an innocuous-looking incident where he twisted his leg, and it effectively ended his career just when it was taking off. He was club captain and in the England Under-21 squad when he was injured. He courageously tried to come back, going through rehabilitation alone for a year, but, tragically, his ligament snapped again. He is now working as a trainee physiotherapist at Maine Road and will no doubt put the same drive and energy that he devoted to his playing into his new career.

As I said, the day was to be filmed, and the resultant programme was shown a few weeks later on satellite TV. While it was happening I couldn't see how they would make something watchable out of it. Firstly, it was a freezing cold day, and secondly, the United men had been out for a further celebration of their League triumph the night before. I had to get enough of my fellow professionals out of their beds early to get started. All of them turned up, for which I was very grateful. David May, Phil and Gary Neville (having found the bunk bed ladder), Paul Scholes, Nicky Butt and Deadly Denis Irwin are all keen golfers, though squad members are banned from playing during the season in case it exhausts them. The Gaffer played in a foursome with Sir Bobby Charlton, Francis Lee and Alan Hill, the City coach. My partner was Niall Quinn, who had left aside his disappointment at Sunderland's relegation to give his support to Paul.

There were some decent golfers playing. Peter Beagrie was the star, but the most remarkable round of the day was put together by our supremo. It may not have been the best, but it was certainly the quickest. I was coming up to the fourth tee by the time the manager had reached the sixteenth green. With the aid of a motorized buggy he whipped around, as he was booked to go and pick up his Carling Manager of the Year Award. You wouldn't have been able to pick up many tips from his showing. Ewen Murray, the professional golfer who was providing part of the commentary, gave him a bit of coaching to try to correct his cramped swing. I'm not sure the Gaffer was having any of it. He believes he is a very good player and probably attributed his woeful performance to the unseemly haste with which he had to proceed. Not that I would ever criticize his golfing technique in any way. My job is to applaud and occasionally remark, "Great shot, Gaffer!" while losing to him.

The rest of the entertainment lay in watching everyone being blown about by the wind. The TV programme broke the monotony by interspersing scenes of players freezing to death with shots of ducks and ducklings suffering in a similar manner. The Shrigley Hall course appeared to have a microclimate all its own. It is atop the one hill in Cheshire, and this might have something to do with it. As I was developing hypothermia and was only standing on the first tee, I put my hands into the pockets of the nice red jackets provided by the sponsors to try fruitlessly to warm them up. It was then that I discovered I had Maureen's car keys with me. I immediately phoned her up to confess and ask if she needed them urgently. She asked me how things were going, and I told her how cold it was there. "It's a beautiful day here," she remarked – a surprise, as we only live about a mile away.

Manchester City emerged victorious. (They have to do it sometime, I suppose, if only by the law of averages). Kit Symons rounded off the day by hitting a duck right at the end. One can only wonder in what circumstances a programme would be made about a group of women engaged in a similar activity, whereas the doings of male sportsmen are always deemed to be so fascinating.

That evening all my family, several of the players and a number of fans who had paid for the privilege came to my wonderfully titled "Gala Ball" at the Palace Hotel in Manchester. Where I'm concerned these evenings never turn out quite as they are supposed to. We were piped in and there was a cabaret, the same one that the team had after one of their Cup final victories. I couldn't remember exactly what they were like, but the muzak which was played at the beginning didn't bode very well for the rest of the evening. We sat down to dinner but afterwards things began to slip out of control. There is something the English find intrinsically comic about national dress (as they don't really have one of their own) and music. A section of the males in Maureen's and my family were wearing that most amusing of garments, the kilt. The entertainers dragged all of them on to the stage and had them putting on an exhibition of what approximated Scots country dancing. This wasn't what the relatives were expecting, and people began to hide under tables to avoid being dragged out of their seats. Because of the hectic nature of the end of the season, for some reason I never seemed to have got round to fixing up a kilt of my own to wear, so was exempt from the public humiliation. All I had to do was enjoy it.

Meanwhile there was an incident in the lift. Beforehand I'd met a couple of men in the bar, one of whom was a very good friend of Eric Cantona's from Leeds. He is actually a Leeds fan but fell in love with Eric when he came to Elland Road. Eric used to get him tickets for games. When Howard Wilkinson sold Eric fatefully to Manchester United, this man was so upset by the sale that he refunded his season ticket and followed Eric across the Pennines to Old Trafford. This wasn't out of any change in allegiance, as supporting one team is hardly compatible with supporting the other. He attends all United's games, and he's also been over to France to watch Eric when he was still an international. The Cantona fan was there along with some acquaintances of mine from Birmingham, and I bought them all a drink. Later on in the evening Chris, the testimonial organizer, came rushing up and said, "Guess what I've just seen?" We'd had a wooden promotional board, a sign, made for these events with a collage of photographs of myself, Maureen and the kids on it. It was really heavy, and not exactly what you would describe as a desirable object. My three chums were busy trying to manhandle it into the lift, trying I presume to make away with it. Chris went up to Eric's admirer and asked him what he was doing. His reply was, "It's nothing to do with me, it was those two's idea."

Then an Irishman who had been very effusive earlier on in the evening came over. He'd previously been saying to me things like, "Choccy, I really love you. I think you've been a great player" – past tense – "and hope you stay here" and so on. He posed for a photo with Maureen and me before we went into dinner. He stood up and sang a song with the band and won one of the prizes, getting well into the party spirit. But when he later came over, he went straight up to one of my friends and asked him, "Choccy, you lovely fella, can I have my picture taken with you?"

My mate stared at him for a while before saying, "Erm... I'm not Brian. That's him over there," indicating where I was standing, only a few yards away.

"No!" He was insistent. "Stop trying to have me on. I know what Brian McClair looks like, I'm his biggest fan, and you're definitely Brian McClair! I want my picture taken with you, and I'm not going till I get it." I could have told my friend that sometimes in these situations it is just better to give in gracefully, as you'll never be around when the pictures come back from the developers.

A similar incident happened to me when I was still playing in Scotland, twelve or thirteen years ago. I'd dropped into a bar after a round of golf with a friend when an old man came up to us and said, "D'ye wanna sign that, Brian?" and handed my golf partner a scrap of paper. He waited till the old man had gone back to the bar and slid it over to me, whispering, "You'd better do this, I think!" Later on, when my friend went to buy another round, the barman rounded on him, saying, "Ah saw what ye did. So ye think yir enough of a superstar not tae have tae sign yir ain autographs anymore. Tha's terrible, that is, getting yir pal tae sign fir that auld guy!" And nothing my friend said could do anything to save my reputation as being unspoilt by what passed for stardom, in that particular pub, anyway. There was absolutely no way the barman would accept that I was Brian McClair.

David May came up to me when I was talking to my brother and (even though he did actually manage to sort out which was his team mate) announced, "Just think, Choccy, you'll look just like him in four years time!" I knew the evening had run its natural course and it would be time to go home soon. My brother soon put him right.

"I'm only twenty nine," he pointed out indignantly.

"Maysie," I cut in at an attempt at salvaging the situation, when I'd stopped laughing. "I accept there may be a resemblance, but not that I look eight years younger." David was past all understanding.

Manchester United had one more game to play before we could either go off on our holidays, or off to Le Tournoi in France. David Busst is the Coventry defender who broke his leg so appallingly in the 1995/96 season and had to leave the game prematurely as the damage sustained and the surgery necessary to heal it was so severe. He had his own testimonial game. I met up with David, who told me that there had been reports in the paper that touts would be offering tickets for the sell-out game. Coventry had avoided the drop by another last-ditch effort, which meant a double reason for their fans to show their support. It would be their biggest home gate of the season. I imagine that, if the United supporters had known what was to be announced later, they might have been paying over the odds for tickets in their hundreds.

Kiddo was in charge of the team for this fixture and he basically intended to give everyone a game. In the first half the fit senior players would make their appearance, and they would go off at half-time. The Coventry team was graced by Paul Gascoigne, who had trimmed himself down and had a getting-down-to-business haircut that signified how much he wanted to retain his England place. He really bustled around and played for the whole match. Les Ferdinand also guested. The usual extreme weather conditions prevailed and it bucketed down. At half-time I went off as planned, but almost immediately Ole Solskjaer injured his leg stretching for a ball so I was hustled back on just as I was beginning to relax. By that time, Gordon Strachan had come on and Steve Ogrizovic was playing as a striker – or that was the theory, anyway. Is it the fantasy of every goalkeeper to be a hot-shot outfield player? Peter would probably have loved to have joined him. They could have circled each other like two massive creatures from *The Lost World*, the pitch shaking beneath their tread.

As far as the score went, Eric Cantona equalized after Gascoigne scored the first goal of the game for Coventry, and then put us into the lead with a penalty. Naturally, tradition dictated that the score could not remain like that (we were not adopting the Celtic model), and it had already been decided that we should give away a penalty in the second half and David Busst would come on to take it. For roughly fifteen minutes we strove manfully to concede the spot kick. Ironically for Leicester fans, Mike Reed, the referee, was reluctant to penalize us. Gary Neville quite enjoyed himself committing a number of clear penalty fouls, obstructions, shirt-tugging and so on, and was amazed that no infringements were signalled. As the end of the match drew close, Gordon Strachan was on the ball, dribbling it away from the box to take it wide for a cross, but also away from any possible penalty-inducing tackles. I decided it was time for me to do something.

"Wee man," I reminded him, "we're supposed to be giving away a penalty here, remember?"

"Aye, yes," he replied. "Sorry, you're right, Choccy, I completely forgot. Foul me or something."

"It's no good from out there."

"Oh, aye! I see what you mean."

Strach went to put the cross over, and by now I had decided I had to do something so conspicuous that there was no possibility of my actions being missed or considered accidental by Mike Reed being in a charitable mood as it was a friendly. As the ball winged across, I rose like a swallow in the box to bat the ball away with my hand. At last, the whistle blew and the referee pointed to the spot.

Not everyone had cottoned on. A friend in the crowd told me later that someone sitting next to them turned round and said, "Do you think he meant to do that?" David Busst despatched the penalty low and hard into the corner of the net. We had to be thankful that Raimond was in goal by that point, as Peter would probably have tried to save it. The match finished there and then. There were many things to enjoy about this evening, but I suppose the best had to be the Coventry support. At the end of the evening, the Coventry escape committee walked round the pitch to loud applause, led by Gordon. He had had the pleasure of playing alongside his eldest son for a brief while. That was very difficult to believe.

Eric Cantona took part for the full ninety minutes. Later some people found a significance in his not being substituted at half-time like other first-teamers, as if he wanted to play it all. But I don't think the romantic viewpoint holds water, as it was really a fluke of the squad members who were available for his position. Only one person there, Eric himself, knew that the Manchester United fans who had come to support David Busst's night would receive what you might call an unexpected bonus, the opportunity to witness his last game for the club. Like everyone else in the team, I found out the next Sunday while I was on holiday with the family in Arran. I'd taken the kids out to swing some golf clubs around and make a lot of noise while Maureen kindled the fire in peace. We'd been back about an hour before she suddenly said, "I knew there was something I meant to tell you. I heard some news on the radio that might interest you." She asked me what I thought about it and I had to say that I was not at all surprised by the announcement that he was leaving Manchester United. What did surprise me was the statement that he was retiring from football altogether. In what might be termed the broader canvas of Eric's life and career to date, this was not such an unusual departure. As he once said, "A football club is like a woman. One leaves when one has nothing else to say..." I wish I could make deeply profound statements like that, but Maureen would never let me get away with spouting such sexist twaddle. The best verdict on his leaving is probably the one borrowed from Douglas (*Hitchhikers' Guide to the Galaxy*) Adams's dolphins, "So long, and thanks for all the fish..."

As I said earlier, there had been a bit of an atmosphere surrounding Eric for a few weeks or so. It's very easy to be wise after the event, as it all seems so obvious afterwards. He was clearly very preoccupied and often seemed sunk in his own thoughts. There was patently something troubling him, but what it was no one in the dressing room could fathom. We won't know what his "retirement" actually consists of for a few months. This is the bit I really can't take seriously, but time may prove me wrong. I've certainly felt like retiring at the end of a season – for the summer perhaps, or maybe even just a week – but once you've had a few weeks' break you see things very differently and are raring to go again. While you still can, you must want to go out on the pitch and play. I can't see that you can lose your love for the game while you still have so much of your fitness and ability. I shouldn't think that this will be the end of his playing career.

As for the timing of his announcement, I appreciate that some feel Eric should have given the supporters the opportunity to see his last game in large numbers, but logistically, when could he have done it? Suppressing the selfish thought that he could have dramatically announced it before my "Gala Ball", where we were raffling the shirt he wore against Dortmund, if you look closely at the other possible occasions, none of them was what you call perfect for the announcement. It would have been rather melodramatic to announce it at the last game of the season, putting a dampener very firmly on the occasion and elevating yourself to a greater importance than the club's success. That also would have gone down well with those who had just spent £40 or £50 on Cantona merchandise for their children or themselves. Perhaps he can come back and do the cash dash draw at half-time one Saturday!

Eric's departure left me thinking about the news from other friends in the game about their future plans. John Colquhoun had signed for St Johnstone for the last eight weeks or so of the season and they won promotion. The manager asked him if he would stay at the club. They wouldn't be able to guarantee that he would play in every game, but he would have a valuable input. But he said no, and told me that he wanted to retire and concentrate on football journalism.

"You can't give up playing," I told him. "Join a pub team or something."

"A pub team? Look, Brian, most pub teams north of the border are playing in the Scottish First Division."

I suggested he might go and play for my home town team, Airdrie, but he wasn't keen. I took Liam there to see their new stadium in a "this is your heritage, my boy" kind of gesture, but he wasn't overly impressed. He's seen Old Trafford and, like many people before him, it has rather spoiled him for anywhere else. Perhaps the same is true for John. He grew up watching United, as his father played for Oldham and he lived in England until he was ten.

One of the things I couldn't really cope with about having a testimonial year was that everything written about me began to sound like an obituary. "You've had a great career but..."; "There must be many memories..." What you want to say is, "Don't bury me yet. I hope there'll be a few more." The important thing is to maintain your appetite.

I do remember one footballer I knew at Celtic who absolutely hated the game, loathed every minute of being on the training round and the football pitch. He founded a small, exclusive clique, the FAF – Footballers Against Football. His main ambition was to find something else that could give him a decent living besides professional football, and, as soon as he found it, he was off.

I was pleased to be able to play for the number of matches I did in 1996/97, including the second half of the Juventus game in Turin, where I don't think I gave a bad account of myself. If we had laid out our priorities at the start of the season and were being realistic, we probably would have said that we wanted to do well in Europe, but that our main aim in terms of what was achieveable would be to win the Premier League. Since United and Arsenal won the Cup Winners' Cup in 1991 and 1992, British teams have hardly been setting Europe alight with either their performances or results. However, having come so close to the Champions' League final and then watching Dortmund pull off a surprise in that competition, we felt disappointed.

15

Here, there and everywhere

"Go and have a run–out there, Brian!"

Twelve thirty a.m., Tuesday 22 July 1997, and I was doing part of my pre-season training sitting in a toilet in Tokyo. Jet lag had afflicted me with a vengeance, just as it did when we flew to Malaysia a couple of years ago. This time I had a plan to deal with it: I had decided I would sleep whenever I felt like it. Consequently, I remember nothing about the flight from Hong Kong to Japan, since I had fallen into oblivion the moment I was settled on the plane. At the hotel I went straight to my room, slept through dinner, and then woke around midnight, refreshed and alert, when everyone else was tucked up happily in their beds. Though Karel was so sound asleep that probably nothing could wake him, I had to observe room-sharing etiquette. A bath took up only fifteen minutes, so my solitary vigil in the wee small hours had to be spent on the only seat available. This is what you travel to other countries for, to broaden the mind. I had never seen a toilet seat quite like it. It heated up and performed a number of other functions that I was afraid to try in case I gave myself a horrific injury and Karel was roused by moaning from the smallest room. While CNN was showing on the tiny television thoughtfully provided for users, I took the opportunity to read over the proofs of the first version of this book. I'd forgotten many of the jokes and found my own wit highly amusing. So my Czech mate's repose was punctuated instead by the sound of his roomie's distant cackling. I trust this was not the reason he signed for Benfica later in the season.

Strange beds and evenings that are empty without children to play with and put to bed mean that, increasingly, when I'm on tour, I don't sleep. Though training makes you physically tired your mind goes on working; well, mine does, anyway. Given the choice I wouldn't have a roommate at all. Not because I'm antisocial, but because I'd like to be able to organize my own evenings and write and read late if it suits me. Karel's departure means that I room with any waif or stray who draws the short straw: Kevin Pilkington, Denis Irwin. I don't have the responsibility of improving their English, just giving it a little maintenance now and again. Denis thought I was always ignoring him at first when he asked me questions, but I'd become accustomed to not talking to anyone. As I pointed out, "Oh, sorry Denis, I didn't realize you were talking to me. I thought it was someone talking in Czech down the phone."

Despite my previous comments about pre-season tours to hot climes, I was more than happy to be sweating it out with the rest on the three-leg Far Eastern tour of Thailand, Hong Kong and Japan. More exciting countries where we see only the stadiums and the plumbing! I did get the chance to visit a mall in Hong Kong looking for presents for the family but failed to find anything suitable. I was fascinated by the Chinese holistic medicine emporia, packed to the roof with exotic nostrums and potions. Most of the remedies appeared to deal with male potency, or so I judged from the names in English on the jars like, "Wild Stallion". I presume the copious instructions in Chinese characters translated as, "If this doesn't work, try conversation".

Whenever we trained there were hundreds of fanatical United fans watching us. For example, there were two thousand or so in the Thai National Stadium, and they cheered loudly as we went through our programme. All the implications of touring in such a different climate had been considered. On the Malaysian tour we became so exhausted that we lost completely the benefit of the week or so's work we had done beforehand and our tiredness affected the start of the season. We returned from our adventures this pre-season having won every game, and having continued with our training effectively. We were unscathed by injury, though I had lost the most weight of all the squad. There is probably a good reason for that. The only problems were encountered by those who considered that they had bartered successfully for bargains in Hong Kong. I remember Phil Neville buying a "Swiss" watch when he toured with England. It never worked, and I helpfully pointed out that they had seen him coming.

"It's under guarantee," he retorted indignantly.

"Send it back then!" I told him, "But how do you know it's genuine?"

"It's in a real box!" Phil announced triumphantly.

Our Norwegians returned with camera lenses which they had haggled up to only double the price you'd pay for them in this country. I could just imagine doing that. "No, no, that's far too cheap – I can afford much more than that!"

"Things Can Only Get Better" was one anthem for this year and, in Manchester United's case at least, that promise has been kept. Following more friendlies against Inter Milan and Slavia Prague and the Charity Shield, we won our league games without playing with any real fluency in August and the first half of September. Strange that the matches against the Italian club were part payment for a player we sold to them, and had since been sold on to Liverpool (some Norwegian-type bargaining at work there, maybe). Though against Chelsea I once again provided the punchline for the old joke, "What is taken to Wembley every year and never used?", I turned out in some of these games and continued to put myself high in the ratings of the Pontin's Fantasy League, courtesy of my assists and even goals (all of three) for the Reserves. Since the last rites were read over my playing career monotonously in my testimonial year, I have hardly managed to have a day off this season, and seem never to have been busier at the club.

We normally come in for training on Sunday morning only if we have a European game midweek, but as I now train with both the Reserves and the first team, and the Reserves usually play on Monday, I am in every Sunday, anxious to show my egalitarianism by not having special treatment. On several Thursdays I followed up my initial coaching training with a course leading to the UEFA B licence at the Cliff, where one of my classes was Injury Recognition. I can now, with confidence, walk up to any of my colleagues lying stricken on the pitch and confirm that he has, in fact, been injured. Added to my book-signing sessions – one, during the course of which I signed a solitary book – and my media appearances, one, on Granada's Footy Show, I barely had a moment. The Footy Show goes out live, and in the course of the programme I shed almost as many pounds as I did in the Far East because of my nervousness, though I enjoyed myself enormously.

It occurred to me, just before we went on air, that I could, in theory, say absolutely anything I wanted and it couldn't be edited out. The thought distracted me mightily throughout the show. As I was answering the questions acceptably one way with my mouth, simultaneously a parallel, outrageous answer formed in my brain which I couldn't give voice to. I'd already told the presenter that I was going to answer his questions with a monosyllabic "yes" or "no", since I like to create a relaxed working atmosphere wherever I go. There I was making my own job more difficult in addition. Still, the programme went well, despite the temptations from my inner demons. Sometimes it's hard to ignore their promptings, especially when they urge me to tackle someone when I come on as sub, or, as happened when I was in the audience for the BBC Sports Personality of the Year, to stand up and scream. Still, I sensed most of the audience had a similar feeling after the first ten minutes.

Our new Champions' League campaign began in Kosice and it was here that I was proud to discover that years of reading Choccy's Diary had rubbed off on United's travelling support. In the seventy-fifth minute, when our contingent was becoming rather bored as the match was all but won after two goals from Denis and Henning Berg, I made an appearance in place of David Beckham. Our fans demonstrated that they have learnt what irony is by the reception they gave me. During the next fifteen minutes they ran through every current song substituting my name for the usual suspect's. "Twelve Brian McClairs", "Brian McClair Running Down the Wing" were two of the offerings, as well as my "own" song, "He's here, he's there, he's every ****ing where!". It made me smile. It is always good to hear your name sung, on whatever basis, and it warmed up a bitterly cold evening.

The Kosice away win had been comfortable, but it was followed by a stutter in our Premier League form with draws at Bolton and against Chelsea, and a rare defeat away to Leeds. Roy Keane's season effectively ended at Elland Road. Even he couldn't run off cruciate ligament damage. "Going through the motions" was a frequent description of the first team's attitude in the press, as if players deliberately say to themselves at the beginning of a season in which they have every prospect of winning the English League, "We'll just go out there today and do enough."

Then came the game where everything seemed to gel. October began with our first encounter with Juventus, at home. Talented sports people can usually achieve a high level of performance but they have occasions when, for some reason, they go beyond that. After the Juventus game fans and journalists were one in saying that the team should be playing like that all the time, that it should go on doing exactly what it did in that match. But it was a one-off performance. It's impossible for a player of any sport to define what it is that makes them outstanding at certain times, just as it is impossible (as I said earlier) to put your finger on the factors that make you play badly.

I reflected gloomily at the end of last season that the team couldn't expect to progress so far in the Champions' League again, so I am happy to report that I have been proved wrong by our largely unhindered progress to the quarter-finals. Winning five out of the six preliminary games surpassed everyone's expectations. And it was a surprise to win so comfortably in most cases, though we were happy with the group when the draw was made. Juventus weren't as strong as they had been in the previous two years, though it would have been better for us to have secured their exit in the final game by beating them, but they really did deserve to win against us in Turin. In the end their triumph was achieved by a late goal from Inzaghi, but in truth they could have been four goals up before then. We have also been luckier this year, so far. But I wish I could shake off the pessimism that descends whenever I think about the Champions' League. I can't help being reminded constantly of the Dortmund games. Celtic beat Rangers convincingly on 2 January, but, in the midst of my euphoria, the sight of Paul Lambert on the pitch cast a dark shadow. Paul is the proud possessor of a European Champions' League Winner's medal with Dortmund, which he left to join my old team. Liverpool have also signed Riedle, who scored two goals in the Champions' League Final in 1997, and mention of his name evokes the same emotion.

In the Premier League we seemed to have finally discovered the knack of winning games by a large margin. For years the Gaffer has been predicting that we would reflect our dominance of games in the scoreline. He was always disappointed by our failure to do so, except on a few memorable occasions like the 5–0 victory over Manchester City, or the 9–0 against Ipswich. By the end of November we had scored four goals or more four times, and beaten Liverpool by three goals to one. One of those victories came against a Blackburn team who, under Roy Hodgson, hadn't lost a game until they met us at Old Trafford. The competition between our forwards undoubtedly made a major contribution. Solskjaer, Sheringham and particularly Andy Cole all looked like scoring at any time and were trying to make it as difficult as possible for the manager to leave them out of the team.

I am very pleased that my previous prophecy about Andy Cole has been fulfilled. After our home game against Feyenoord, people outside the club had written him off and were busy drawing up lists of the forwards United were about to sign in his stead. But as soon as he was fit enough to play with the sharpness and acceleration his type of game demands, the goals flowed. Butt and Scholes have played with maturity in midfield, Paul continuing to demonstrate the qualities he showed at international level. Nicky has risen to the challenge of more responsibility in midfield. In a practice game he proudly accepted leadership of the younger players by wrapping a piece of tape round his arm and inscribing it, "Capten". Ryan Giggs's form followed on from his excellent play last season, which seemed to have slipped to the back of people's minds because he ended it with an injury.

The Blackburn tie rounded off a highly successful November, spoiled only by a second League defeat by Arsenal. Once again, when I replaced Teddy Sheringham with fifteen minutes left to play, the whole repertoire of new Brian McClair songs rang out, with the addition of loud cheers whenever I touched the ball. It was a bit of a shock to hear it at Old Trafford, since there were so many thousands more fans joining in the collective irony than in Czechoslovakia.

In my diary for the magazine I like to include stories that run through several issues. My readers have been enthralled by the gripping tale of the two rabbits and guinea pig that Maureen and I bought for the weans. I am constantly striving for ways to improve their environment and have even employed my woodworking skills to build a run and a hutch separator to protect the guinea pig from the unwelcome attentions of his bunny "friends". These include continually peeing on the poor thing's food and water. In fact, the only way that I could better their living conditions would be to move them into the house and give them their own bedroom. According to one of my acquaintances who was listening to the fun at the Blackburn game on the radio, Alan Green observed that the Gaffer was fortunate because United were so comfortable he could turn round to Brian McClair and say, "Go and have a run-out there, Brian!", in a striking parallel between me and the rabbits. At least I neither attempted to jump over the North Stand nor got wedged between the corner flags and the billboards and tried to dig myself out. I also kept well away from the drinks bottles. I made our fourth and last goal for the Blackburn defender Jeff Kenna by rolling the ball forward for him to tuck it past Flowers.

We had what appeared to be a very satisfactory December and Christmas programme, topping the Premier League courtesy of another three victories. One of these was against Everton, where I again played the last quarter of an hour for Pally, after warming up for seventy-five minutes or so. At least our festive season was satisfactory until, on 28 December, we boarded the coach for Coventry.

The organization of our coach is very territorial. Like the creatures of habit that we are, we tend to sit in the same places and do pretty much the same things. I usually sit with Kiddo at the front, talking nonsense for a few hours. Kiddo has a wealth of topics on which he likes to hold forth at length. Though I have never been to the Lake District I feel I know every puddle and stone. Kiddo has a place there which he intends to have done up when he can afford it and which he visits when time allows. He's even got to the stage where he draws maps for me. Occasionally he intersperses his eulogies of Windermere and Grasmere with appreciations of the recordings of Frank Sinatra. I sometimes attempt to cut in with the outrageous suggestion that Scotland also has some very beautiful scenery, but am not allowed to develop this theme at any length before Kiddo is back on his tarns.

Across the aisle sit Dave Fevre, Ken Merrett and Peter Schmeichel. Peter always wants to play cards but every time he suggests a game there is the same exchange between these passengers. Dave tells Peter that he has work to do; Ken says he doesn't want to play cards. Kiddo is needed to make up the foursome and is prepared to have "one quick game". Then they play Aces to Kings for the whole journey, as you know they are going to all along. Kiddo never pauses in his educative geographical or musical monologue, while cheating blatantly. Directly behind us sit the brats: Giggs, Butt, Scholes, the Nevilles. They occupy their time usefully by throwing sweeties and screwed-up bits of paper at each other and disturbing their elders with their racket. We discourage them from playing with their Gameboys because they fall out over them and I have to step in and confiscate their machines when they can't play nicely.

The galley divides our coach in two between the sages and pups at the front, and the foreign section and the card school in the rear. Ronnie, Ole, Jordi, Henning and Raimond play games too, but with a serious purpose, as Raimond wants to be a pilot and brings a flight-simulation exercise. The Gaffer, Denis, Pally and Teddy are the gamblers. The Gaffer is especially keen because he wins more often since Bryan Robson departed to manage Middlesbrough. Our manager never worked out (well, I presume he didn't) that Robbo, Steve Bruce and Pally had a conspiracy to ensure that he never won. "I'm paying out all the time," he'd mutter darkly, mystified by his lengthy losing streak.

Card playing is not the attraction it once was for our squad. I recall that in my early days at the club Arthur Albiston and Kevin Moran used to play. Arthur had elaborate systems and the phenomenal knack of remembering every card he had put down. He never won though.

When all else fails, and we are too tired to distract ourselves, collective entertainment is provided in the form of a video. It's usually the case that we are all too bone idle to go to the shop and get one, so we have to watch the few tapes that have been donated to the bus over and over again – some episodes of Only Fools and Horses and The Bodyguard.

On our way to the Midlands some of the drivers making the same journey were indulging in their favourite sport: "Oh look, there's the United coach behind us. Slam the brakes on!" A wee bit tedious when it happens for the eighth time in the driving rain. Coventry engaged in a similar activity when we reached Highfield Road, slowing down United's progress at the top of the Premier League and confounding those who had declared the contest over before the New Year was welcomed in. Two goals in the last five minutes gave the Sky Blues victory, one a penalty and the other a great individual effort from Huckerby. "Complacency," screamed the headlines, but that ignores the fact that Coventry made us uncomfortable throughout and we weren't defending well enough to neutralize the threat of Huckerby's pace and Dublin's aerial ability.

I don't believe, as I've said before, that United ever approach a game with the arrogant attitude our critics gleefully denounce, but I do think that it is difficult to regain your momentum if you lose it. A match can easily slip away from you if that happens. However, our first half-drubbing of Chelsea 5-0 in the third round of the FA Cup at the beginning of the New Year was nearly lost by a rare demonstration of complacency. A few attempted tricks and clever balls from our men were seized on to good effect by Le Saux and Vialli and Chelsea came so near to closing the gap to 5–4 with only a few minutes left.

The press had decided by Christmas, as I said earlier, that the Premier League was dead as a competition and the silverware was firmly in United's grasp. We took a very different view of events. The Gaffer gave an interview in which he reiterated the point that realistically you can afford to lose only six games if you want to win the Premiership. (The only exception to that equation was in 1995 when Blackburn lost seven games, but we as the second team drew too many matches.) We subsequently lost the next two games to Southampton and Leicester, each by a 1–0 scoreline. In the second half of both ties we achieved the seemingly impossible – not scoring at least one goal from the endless series of chances that came our way. These two "shock" defeats were punctuated by the equally shocking sight of Brian McClair playing for the whole of a first-team game in the 5–1 FA Cup fourth-round victory against Walsall. This was part of the manager's strategy for surviving the heavy fixture programme that our continued success in three competitions would create later in the season. There can be no calls for an extension of the season this year because of the World Cup. My FA Cup involvement has already survived longer than my run-out in the Coca-Cola Cup, which ended with a 2–0 defeat by Ipswich in October.

Liam is learning how to read and car journeys are now accompanied by continual demonstrations of his new skill. He was busy reading the signs we passed on the way to the ground for the Cup tie.

"Keep... out. Keep out, Dad! No... left turn."

"That's very good, son, I'm glad you're learning to read..."

"Yes, Dad."

"...because then you can go on to secondary school, pass all your exams..."

"Yes, Dad."

"...go on to uni or get a good job..."

"Yes, Dad."

"...and leave home!"

"Yes, Dad." Liam continued to agree, unabashed. "And then you'll be able to go to church every day, not just on Sunday."

"Erm, I'm afraid you're going to have to explain that one to me, Liam."

"Like Granny, Dad."

So this is how my son sees my future. Once I've finished raising him all I'll have left to fill my time is trundling to Mass every day.

Sometimes the finer points of fatherhood can escape me. Liam won't stay in bed and comes downstairs to join his mum and me when we're watching a film. Last night's offering was quite violent and Maureen spent most of the time covering his eyes at unsuitable moments. Of course, Liam kept asking, "What's going on now?" and I obliged by filling him in on the action: "They've just chopped all his fingers off!" Maureen informed me that the definition of parental guidance is not that your dad describes in graphic detail all the nasty bits you're not allowed to see. She decided that our son should go back upstairs and tried to still his complaints by pointing out that he would be able to watch these films when he grew up. "But they'll all be in black and white then!" he moaned.

Lawrence Donegan, a journalist and an ex-schoolmate of John Colquhoun, has written a very funny book about golfing. I mention it here because, on page four, he says that I stole his destiny, becoming the professional footballer for Celtic and United that he always wanted to be. Lawrence was a member of Lloyd Cole and the Commotions, a band which had notable hits, the most famous of which is probably Perfect Skin. This amused Colquhoun and me greatly, because the standard fantasy indulged in by most footballers is that if they weren't players they would be rock stars. So, while every young male rocker appears to be anxious to turn out in five-a-sides and charity matches, we professionals all want to be fronting our own bands. Lee Sharpe, I remember, had a drum kit which he leathered unrhythmically in half-hearted pursuance of this dream. On the whole it's better just to stick at what you do well. And before anyone says anything, the latest, woeful chart offering from this club, "Sing Up for the Champions", can't be pinned on me. The lyrics of some terrace standards were altered to make them suitable for the ears of the general public. I still wait to be enlightened about why "Roy Keane is magic" couldn't be tolerated and became, "Roy Keane is a demon".

The other United team I play for has not emulated the previous season's successes so far. Maybe I won't be polishing another Pontin's League winner's medal come May. The Reserves are arguably in a state of transition. Some of the regulars from last season have been sold to other clubs, Michael Appleton and John O'Kane, for example. Others have made the leap into the first team. We also appear to be facing stronger opposition, perhaps as a result of the expansion of other clubs' squads. In August we were beaten 3–0 by Leeds Reserves. The much-maligned Tomas Brolin came on to score two goals and Tony Yeboah gave our young defenders problems. But the important thing, as far as our club is concerned, is to develop our young players in the right way.

February began with a formal remembrance of another team of young United players. The fortieth anniversary of the Munich air crash, which killed twenty-three men, eight of them United footballers, was marked by a service at Manchester Cathedral and a small ceremony in the middle of the pitch. Eight wreaths were laid in the centre circle and the players formed a line with linked arms and heads bowed. The silence was observed immaculately and was a moving and restrained tribute. There are several football clubs in this country that have been linked with some form of tragedy. Bolton Wanderers, our opponents on the day, lost supporters in a fire at Burnden Park, their old home. Manchester United fans will always feel that the Munich crash entitles the club to a special place in football's history. Feelings of loss and regret for the unfulfilled promise of players like Duncan Edwards, Tommy Taylor, Eddie Colman and the rest go hand in hand with admiration for the courage of those who survived and went on to rebuild the team once more. Matt Busby was one of those rare figures who nobody had a bad word for and who won the respect of everyone. For myself this day was another of those occasions that emphasized what a privilege it is to be associated with a club like this one.

Postscript

Daydream believer

I have always daydreamed and I still do. As a boy, I dreamed constantly about becoming a professional footballer, but the future I imagined for myself would have had a hard time matching the reality. Over the summer, my father retrieved my old tech drawing board, bought when I was doing my O Levels, out of the attic and gave it to me. I hadn't seen it since my teens. It was covered with doodles in red pen. That much I remember. What I hadn't retained is what I scribbled when I was enlivening my homework by drifting off into fantasy. I'd written "Brian McClair", but also, and this is absolutely true, "Man United". Even in my most grandiose moments, I would never have presumed to think that one day I could add: one Scottish Championship, one Scottish FA Cup, a Golden Boot, four Championships, three FA Cups, one European Cup Winners' Cup, one Rumbelow's Cup, one European Super Cup and thirty Scottish Caps.

If anyone had told me when I brought my wife and one-year-old daughter to England in July 1987 that I would be here for eleven years, I would have laughed. I gave myself two years at the most, aware of the Scots who had been hugely successful when they came south, but also of the large numbers who had not lived up to expectations. I believed I would return to Scotland, hoped that I would have had some success. I didn't want to go back an abject failure, and that fear of failing was a major spur. I didn't intend to use it as a stepping stone in my career, because there's no way up from here when you leave; there is nowhere else in England that is better. When you go, it's a step down. One moment I was here in England with one baby; suddenly I've got three children and they're going to school, very settled and, as I said before, believing that they're English. And eleven years have passed by.

One football magazine recently placed me at number ten in their feature, "Twenty managers to look out for" – quite a compliment considering that I haven't managed anything yet. Last year, when the Gaffer confirmed that I would be given a year's extension to my contract, I joked that I might have been kept on to clean the players' cars and dug out my chammy leather. Now I am trying to enjoy every minute and not complicate my life any further by contemplating what my future in the game might be until I absolutely have to. I haven't applied for a single job in my life. I didn't even fill out an application when I went shelf-stacking in the local supermarket after school.

So, in answer to the question "What happens next?" I can only say that I shall save the last section on my laptop and go and make myself a cup of tea while savouring the temporary status I have achieved by becoming a cult. At least I think that was what a bloke in the crowd called me last week.

Fixtures 1996/97

Pre-season friendly, Saturday 27 July, Shamrock Park

Portadown 0, Manchester United 5
Scholes, Scholes, Keane, Beckham, Scholes

Pre-season friendly, Sunday 28 July, Tolka Park

League of Ireland XI 1, Manchester United 4
Gough; Sharpe, Pallister, Scholes, Cantona

Pre-season friendly, Wednesday 31 July, Giuseppe Meazza

Internatazionale 3, Manchester United 1
Carbone, Branca, Branca

Umbro International Tournament, Saturday 3 August, City Ground

Ajax 2, Manchester United 1
Frank de Boer, Kiki Musampa; McClair

Umbro International Tournament, Sunday 4 August, City Ground

Nottingham Forest 1, Manchester United 3
Campbell; Beckham, McClair, Neville

Charity Shield, Sunday 11 August, Wembley

Manchester United 4, Newcastle United 0
Cantona, Butt, Beckham, Keane

Pre-season friendly, Tuesday 15 August, Old Trafford

Manchester United 0, Internazionale 1
Zamorano

Premiership #1, Saturday 17 August, Selhurst Park

Wimbledon 0, Manchester United 3
Cantona, Irwin, Beckham

Premiership #2, Wednesday 21 August, Old Trafford

Manchester United 2, Everton 2
Cruyff, Unsworth; Ferguson, Ferguson

Premiership #3, Sunday 25 August, Old Trafford

Manchester United 2, Blackburn Rovers 2
Cruyff, Solskjaer; Warhurst, Bohinen

Premiership #4, Wednesday 4 September, Baseball Ground

Derby County 1, Manchester United 1
Laursen; Beckham

Premiership #5, Saturday 7 September, Elland Road

Leeds United 0, Manchester United 4
Martyn, Butt, Poborsky, Cantona

Champions' League #1, Wednesday 11 September, Stadio Delle Alpi

Juventus 1, Manchester United 0
Boksic

Premiership #6, Saturday 14 September, Old Trafford

Manchester United 4, Nottingham Forest
Solskjaer, Giggs, Cantona, Cantona; Haaland

Premiership #7, Saturday 21 September, Villa Park

Aston Villa 0, Manchester United 0

Champions' League #2, Wednesday 25 September, Old Trafford

Manchester United 2, SK Rapid Wien 0
Solskjaer, Beckham

Premiership #8, Sunday 29 September, Old Trafford

Manchester United 2, Tottenham Hotspur 0
Solskjaer, Solskjaer

Premiership #9, Saturday 12 October, Old Trafford

Manchester United 1, Liverpool 0
Beckham

Champions' League #3, Wednesday 16 October, Fenerbahçe

Fenerbahçe SK 0, Manchester United 2
Beckham, Cantona

Premiership #10, Sunday 20 October, St James' Park

Newcastle United 5, Manchester United 0
Peacock, Ginola, Ferdinand, Shearer, Albert

Coca-Cola Cup R3, Wednesday 23 October, Old Trafford

Manchester United 2, Swindon Town 1
Poborsky, Scholes; Thorne

Premiership #11, Saturday 26 October, The Dell

Southampton 6, Manchester United 3
Berkovic, Le Tissier, Ostenstad, Berkovic, Ostenstad, Ostenstad; Beckham, May, Scholes

Champions' League #4, Wednesday 30 October, Old Trafford

Manchester United 0, Fenerbahçe 1
Bolic

Premiership #12, Saturday 2 November, Old Trafford

Manchester United 1, Chelsea 2
May; Duberry, Vialli

Premiership #13, Saturday 16 November, Old Trafford

Manchester United 1, Arsenal 0
Winterburn

Champions' League #5, Wednesday 20 November, Old Trafford

Manchester United 0, Juventus 1
Del Piero

Premiership #14, Saturday 23 November, Riverside Stadium

Middlesbrough 2, Manchester United 2
Ravanelli, Hignett; Keane, May

Coca-Cola Cup R4, Wednesday 27 November, Filbert Street

Leicester City 2, Manchester United 0
Claridge, Heskey

Premiership #15, Saturday 30 November, Old Trafford

Manchester United 3, Leicester City 1
Butt, Solskjaer; Lennon

Champions' League #6, Wednesday 4 December, Ernst Happel

SK Rapid Wien 0, Manchester United 2
Giggs, Cantona

Premiership #16, unday 8 December, Boleyn Ground

West Ham United 2, Manchester United 2
Raducioiu, Dicks; Solskjaer, Beckham

Odd Man Out

Premiership #17, Wednesday 18 December, Hilssborough

Sheffield Wednesday 1, Manchester United 1
Carbone; Scholes

Premiership #18, Saturday 21 December, Old Trafford

Manchester United 5, Sunderland 0
Solskjaer, Cantona, Solskjaer, Butt, Cantona

Premiership #19, Thursday 26 December, City Ground

Nottingham Forest 0, Manchester United 4
Beckham, Butt, Solskjaer, Cole

Premiership #20, Saturday 28 December, Old Trafford

Manchester United 1, Leeds United 0
Cantona

Premiership #21, Wednesday 1 January, Old Trafford

Manchester United 0, Aston Villa 0

FA Cup R3, Sunday 5 January, Old Trafford

Manchester United 2, Tottenham Hotspur 0
Scholes, Beckham

Premiership #22, Sunday 12 January, White Hart Lane

Tottenham Hotspur 1, Manchester United 2
Allen; Solskjaer, Beckham

Premiership #23, Saturday 18 January, Highfield Road

Coventry City 0, Manchester United 2
Giggs, Solskjaer

FA Cup R4, Saturday 25 January, Old Trafford

Manchester United 1, Wimbledon 1
Scholes; Earle

Premiership #24, Wednesday 29 January, Old Trafford

Manchester United 2, Wimbledon 1
Giggs, Cole; Perry

Premiership #25, Saturday 1 February, Old Trafford

Manchester United 2, Southampton 1
Pallister, Cantona; Ostenstad

FA Cup R4R, Tuesday 4 February, Selhurst Park

Wimbledon 1, Manchester United 0
Gayle

Premiership #26, Wednesday 19 February, Highbury

Arsenal 1, Manchester United 2
Bergkamp; Cole, Solskjaer

Premiership #27, Saturday 22 February, Stamford Bridge

Chelsea 1, Manchester United 1
Zola; Beckham

Premiership #28, Saturday 1 March , Old Trafford

Manchester United 3, Coventry City 1
Breen, Poborsky, Cole; Huckerby

Champions' League #7, Wednesday 5 March, Old Trafford

Manchester United 4, FC Porto 0
May, Cantona, Giggs, Cole

Premiership #29, Saturday 8 March, Roker Park

Sunderland 2, Manchester United 1
Gray, Mullin; Melville

Premiership #30, Saturday 15 March, Old Trafford

Manchester United 2, Sheffield Wednesday 0
Cole, Poborsky

Champions' League #8, Wednesday 19 March, Estadio das Antas

FC Porto 0, Manchester United 0

Premiership #31, Saturday 22 March, Goodison Park

Everton 0, Manchester United 2
Solksjaer, Cantona

Premiership #32, Saturday 5 April, Old Trafford

Manchester United 2, Derby County 3
Cantona, Solskjaer; Ward, Wanchope, Sturridge

Champions' League SF 1L, Wednesday 9 April, Ernst Happel

Borussia Dortmund 1, Manchester United 0
Tretschok

Premiership #33, Saturday 12 April, Ewood Park

Blackburn Rovers 2, Manchester United 3
Warhurst, McKinlay; Cole, Scholes, Cantona

Premiership #34, Saturday 19 April, Anfield

Liverpool 1, Manchester United 3
Barnes; Pallister, Pallister, Cole

Champions' League SF 2L, Wednesday 23 April, Old Trafford

Manchester United 0, Borussia Dortmund 1
Ricken

Premiership #35, Saturday 3 May, Filbert Street

Leicester City 2, Manchester United 2
Walsh, Marshall; Solskjaer, Solskjaer

Premiership #36, Monday 5 May, Old Trafford

Manchester United 3, Middlesbrough 3
Keane, Neville, Solskjaer; Juninho, Emerson, Hignett

Premiership #37, Thursday 8 May, Old Trafford

Manchester United 0, Newcastle United 0

Premiership #38, Sunday 11 May, Old Trafford

Manchester United 2, West Ham United 0
Scholes, Cruyff

1997/98 season

Charity Shield, Sunday 3 August, Wembley Stadium

Chelsea 1, Manchester United 1
Hughes; Johnsen
Penalties: United won 4–2 (Scholes, Zola, Irwin, Keane, Leboeuf, Butt)

Premiership #1, Sunday 10 August, White Hart Lane

Tottenham Hotspur 0, Manchester United 2
Butt, Vega (own goal)

Premiership #2, Wednesday 13 August, Old Traffford

Manchester United 1, Southampton 0
Beckham

Fixtures

Premiership #3, Saturday 23 August, Filbert Street

Leicester City 0, Manchester United 0

Premiership #4, Wednesday 27 August, Goodison Park

Everton 0, Manchester United 2
Beckham, Sheringham

Premiership #5, Saturday 30 August, Old Trafford

Manchester United 2, Coventry City 0
Cole, Keane

Premiership #6, Saturday 13 September, Old Trafford

Manchester United 2, West Ham United 1
Keane, Scholes; Hartson

Champions' League, Wednesday 17 September, Lokomotiva

FC Kosice 0, Manchester United 3
Irwin, Berg, Cole

Premiership #7, Saturday 20 September, Reebok Stadium

Bolton Wanderers 0, Manchester United 0

Premiership #8, Wednesday 24 September, Old Trafford

Manchester United 2, Chelsea 2
Scholes, Solskjaer; Berg (own goal), Hughes

Premiership #9, Saturday 27 September, Elland Road

Leeds United 1, Manchester United 0
Wetherall

Champions' League, Wednesday 1 October, Old Trafford

Manchester United 3, Juventus 2
Sheringham, Scholes, Giggs; Del Piero, Zidane

Premiership #10, Saturday 4 October, Old Trafford

Manchester United 2, Crystal Palace 0
Sheringham, Hreiderson (own goal)

Coca-Cola Cup Round Three, Monday 13 October, Portman Road

Ipswich Town 2, Manchester United 0
Mathie, Taricco

Odd Man Out

Premiership #11, Saturday 18 October, Pride Park

Derby County 2, Manchester United 2
Baiano, Wanchope, Sheringham, Cole

Champions' League, Wednesday 22 October, Old Trafford

Manchester United 2, SC Feyenoord 1
Scholes, Irwin (pen), Vos

Premiership #12, Saturday 25 October, Old Trafford

Manchester United 7, Barnsley 0
Cole 3, Giggs 2, Scholes, Poborsky

Premiership #13, Saturday 1 November, Old Trafford

Manchester United 6, Sheffield Wednesday 1
Sheringham 2, Cole 2, Solskjaer 2; Whittingham

Champions' League, Wednesday 5 November, De Kuyp

SC Feyenoord 1, Manchester United 3
Korneev; Cole 3

Premiership #14, Sunday 9 November, Highbury

Arsenal 3, Manchester United 2
Anelka, Vieira, Platt; Sheringham 2

Premiership #15, Saturday 22 November, Selhurst Park

Wimbledon 2, Manchester United 5
Ardley, M Hughes; Butt, Beckham 2, Scholes, Cole

Champions' League, Thursday 27 November, Old Trafford

Manchester United 3, FC Kosice 0
Cole, Sheringham, Faktor (own goal)

Premiership #16, Sunday 30 November, Old Trafford

Manchester United 4, Blackburn Rovers 0
Solskjaer 2, Henchoz (own goal), Kenna (own goal)

Premiership #17, Saturday 6 December, Anfield

Liverpool 1, Manchester United 3
Fowler (pen); Cole 2, Beckham

Champions' League, Wednesday 10 December, Stadio Delle Alpi

Juventus 1, Manchester United 0
Inzaghi

Premiership #18, Monday 15 December, Old Trafford

Manchester United 1, Aston Villa 0
Giggs

Premiership #19, Sunday 21 December, St James' Park

Newcastle United 0, Manchester United 1
Cole

Premiership #20, Friday 26 December, Old Trafford

Manchester United 2, Everton 0
Berg, Cole

Premiership #21, Sunday 28 December, Highfield Road

Coventry City 3, Manchester United 2
Whelan, Dublin (pen), Huckerby; Solskjaer, Sheringham

FA Cup Round Three, Sunday 4 January, Stamford Bridge

Chelsea 3, Manchester United 5
Le Saux, Vialli, Beckham 2, Cole 2, Sheringham

Premiership #22, Saturday 10 January, Old Trafford

Manchester United 2, Tottenham Hotspur 0
Giggs 2

Premiership #23, Monday 19 January 1998, The Dell

Southampton 1, Manchester United 0
Davies

FA Cup Round Four, Saturday 24 January, Old Trafford

Manchester United 5, Walsall 1
Cole 2, Solskjaer 2, Johnsen; Boli

Other titles available from Manchester United Books

☐ 0 233 99154 9	Manchester United Official Review 97/98	£9.99
☐ 0 233 99045 3	Cantona on Cantona	£14.99
☐ 0 233 99047 X	Alex Ferguson: Ten Glorious Years	£9.99
☐ 0 233 99046 1	Ryan Giggs: Genius at Work	£9.99
☐ 0 233 99340 1	Manchester United: The Insider Guide	£7.99
☐ 0 233 99354 9	Sir Matt Busby: A Tribute	
	The Official Authorised Biography	£9.99
☐ 0 233 99368 1	A Will to Win: The Manager's Diary	
	by Alex Ferguson with David Meek	£6.99

Forthcoming titles Autumn 1998:

☐ 0 233 99148 4	David Beckham: My Story	
	by David Beckham with Neil Harman	£12.99
☐ 0 233 99417 3	The Official Manchester United Quiz Book	£7.99
☐ 0 233 99216 2	Manchester United Diary 1999	£4.99

For children and older kids:

☐ 0 233 99374 6	Manchester United Log Book	£4.99
☐ 0 233 99218 9	Manchester United Annual 1999	£5.50

MUFC Pocket Books:

☐ 0 233 99370 3	Manchester United: Great Moments	£4.99
☐ 0 233 99371 1	Manchester United: Life in the Squad	£4.99
☐ 0 233 99372 X	Manchester United: Meet the Players	£4.99
☐ 0 233 99373 8	Old Trafford: Behind the Scenes	£4.99

All these books are available at your local bookshop or can be ordered direct from the publisher. Prices and availability are subject to change without notice.

Send orders to:

Manchester United Cash Sales, 76 Dean Street, London W1V 5HA

Please send a cheque or postal order made payable to VCI plc for the value of the book(s) and add the following for postage and packaging (remembering to give your name and address): *UK:* £1.00 for the first book, 50p for the second and 30p for each additional book up to a maximum of £3.00.

OVERSEAS including EIRE: £2.00 for the first book and £1.00 for the second and 50p for each additional book up to a maximum of £5.00